THE HISTORY OF
SOUTH YORKSHIRE GLASS

by

Denis Ashurst, M.A.

© Denis Ashurst

Publisher: J.R. Collis
Editor   R.B. Adams

*A cataloguing in publication record for this book
is available from the British Library*

ISBN 0 906090 46 6

Copies of this volume and a catalogue of other publications
by the Department of Archaeology & Prehistory,
University of Sheffield can be obtained from:

    J.R. Collis Publications
    Department of Archaeology & Prehistory
    University of Sheffield
    Sheffield S10 2TN
    Phone/Fax 742 797158

Printed in Great Britain by

The Alden Press
Osney Mead, Oxford

To Florence

Contents

Figures

Tables

Acknowledgements

Research for this book has been undertaken over many years and it is a pleasant duty to acknowledge the help received over this time. I am especially grateful to both Rotherham and Barnsley Metropolitan Borough Councils, whose financial aid made the publication possible and to Paul Flintoff, former Keeper of Fine Arts at the Rotherham Museum not only for his enthusiastic support but for permission to make use of his own work on some aspects of the research. My sincere thanks to the many unnamed 'diggers' who gave up their free time to work in all weathers, and also to John Little, County Chief Archaeologist for his support.

Working over the wide field the subject tries to cover must draw upon the labours of others, past and present, and my indebtedness to them is hopefully reflected in the bibliography and notes. I am pleased to record my gratitude for the help and guidance always available to me from David Crossley, Professor David Hey, Professor Michael Cable, Robert Charleston, Ruth Hurst-Vose and John Goodchild.

My wife has contributed greatly to this research not merely in her calm acceptance of the domestic upheavals such work causes but in her accomplishments in recording excavated material and the often remarkable reconstructions she produced. Not least she has been the sternest, yet kindest, of critics. I am indebted to the many archivists and librarians for their assistance, particularly at Rotherham, Barnsley, Sheffield and Wakefield and to the Borthwick Institute of Historical Research. All archaeological material has been deposited at the Sheffield City Museum where I am grateful for use of the facilities of the Conservation Unit.

I am pleased to acknowledge permission to reproduce the following copyright material; Sheffield Archives for quotations from Wood Brothers Day Book and the Fairbank drawing of Attercliffe; Barnsley Local History Archive for the Hope Glassworks illustration; Rotherham Local History Archive for use of the Kilner advertisement together with Beatson Clark for the eighteenth century letterheads and Regulations; exhibits from the University of Sheffield glass collection Figures 10 and 11. Reproductions of the Ashley and the Owen machines are by permission of the Trustees of the Science Museum.

Preface

This study of the South Yorkshire glass industry grew from an interest in recording what had once been a major contributor to the region's prosperity at a time when it was in danger of being totally forgotten. Combining archaeological and historical research it looks into all aspects of the industry's growth and decline over two thousand years particularly in the areas of Barnsley, Rotherham, Sheffield and Doncaster. It illustrates and explains the technological changes in glassmaking in the region, discusses the wide range of products and inventions, especially the role of bottles, and describes the operation of various glassworks with reference to the working conditions of the glassworkers. The Gazetteer provides a full list of all known glassworks in South Yorkshire at all periods (over 60) giving a brief summary of each works and the Ordnance Survey Grid reference where known, in addition to the greater detail in the main text.

Authors' names given as a reference within the text refer to the Bibliography and number references to the Notes for original documentary sources.

All weights, money etc used in the periods covered by the book were, of course, calculated in the old Imperial measures of pre-decimalisation. These have been retained to preserve the realism and conversions have not been added to avoid excessive disruption of the text. The following approximate equivalents of quantities which occur may be useful:

1 mile	=	1.6 km	£1	=	100p
1 yard	=	0.914m	15s	=	75p
1 foot	=	30.5cm	10s	=	50p
1 ton	=	1016kg	8s	=	40p
1 cwt	=	50.8kg	7s 6d	=	37p
1 lb	=	0.45kg	6s	=	30p
1 gallon	=	4.55 l	4d	=	1.7p
			1d	=	0.4p

INTRODUCTION

A world without glass is now inconceivable. A window would still be a hole in a wall which could be covered with cloth to keep out some of the draught, but also kept out the light. Modern plastics which might be thought an adequate substitute could not, of course, have been developed without the glass test tubes and beakers essential to the chemist. Transport would have progressed little beyond the horse and cart as aeroplanes and cars could hardly exist without the protected visibility provided by glass. Communications would still be restricted to the carrier pigeon and semaphore era as even the simplest telegraph depended on glass valves, and from this there could have been no development through the transistor to telephones, radio, television, cinema or computers – all now seen as vital to personal and commercial life in the modern world.

The list seems endless, yet glass also has an inherent quality of beauty bringing another dimension to the art of living. It might be a quite useless ornament that gives simple pleasure to the eye or a delicate wine glass which brings that indefinable quality to even the simplest toast; champagne from an earthenware beaker must surely lose something of its savour.

There is, however, one use for glass which became the very heart of the South Yorkshire glass industry and is, sadly, so taken for granted as to be hardly considered worthy of a second glance, namely the humble and much neglected bottle. The history of the South Yorkshire glass industry is largely the story of bottles and jars, mundane perhaps, but in their way almost as vital to the comforts of modern living as the introduction of glass to the hole in the wall which became a window.

Modern glass technology is extremely complex yet, apart from a few very specialist modern glasses, this most versatile and remarkable material consists basically of one of the commonest substances making up the earth's crust, namely, silica, as sand or flint. A temperature in excess of 1700° C is required to melt silica but the addition of an alkali such as soda or potash will reduce this to around 1100° C bringing it within range of a simple furnace. Lime is added to the silica/alkali mix to stabilise the glass and these three substances, sand/alkali/lime, have formed the basis of all common glass since its obscure discovery in Western Asia some five thousand years ago.

The main impurity in sand is iron oxide which can colour glass in varying degrees of green or brown to almost black. In even the most modern clear window glass the green tinge is visible at the edge of the pane. However, the deliberate colouration of glass appears to have no limits and any colour in any shade can be reproduced by strict control of the furnace conditions and the addition of suitable trace substances, such as cobalt for example to give blue glass (Newton and Davison 1989).

New glass also contains a proportion of old glass, referred to as 'cullet'. This might be from faulty products which have been rejected at the works or from broken glass discarded as public rubbish, hence the emergence of the 'bottle bank'. Even modern glass can require up to 50% of cullet. The bottle bank is more than an attempt to be environmentally friendly; old glass is an essential ingredient of new glass. The cullet is broken up and added to the basic mix to encourage earlier melting and a more homogeneous glass, though coloured waste must obviously not be added to an intended clear glass product.

One variation of this basic mix was perfected by George Ravenscroft in the 1670s and has stood the test of time. This was the creation of 'lead crystal' by the addition of lead oxide (red lead) to the sand/alkali/lime mix to produce a glass intended to rival the Venetian 'cristallo'. Early experiments had used crushed flint instead of sand so giving the name 'flint glass' and, although the glassmakers reverted to using sand, the name stuck and we now have a confusion of 'lead', 'crystal' and 'flint' glass all of which are a mix of sand or flint with soda or potash and lime together with lead oxide, with or without additional colouring. This use of lead oxide to produce a fine glass which has since been in constant demand will be seen to have caused considerable technical problems for the early glassmakers. Recent evidence from South Yorkshire has shown how they were solved.

In fact the history of the South Yorkshire industry since its seventeenth century origins very much reflects the national post-medieval industry with a similar course of events being followed at other major glass producing areas such as the Midlands, Bristol, Newcastle and London in both growth and decline. Changes in glass technology and their effects on the glassworkers, changes in fashion affecting the range of products, new ideas in culinary techniques, even changes in drinking habits – all can be traced through the history of glass production and this book attempts to bring together these varying aspects of the industry.

Excellent books on the general history of glassmaking and glass for collectors have already been written but none has looked in detail at a particular area to see these developments through the eyes of the people involved. In addition there has long been a tendency in all such histories to either omit the role of South Yorkshire entirely or, at best, give it passing mention.

This neglect is strange in view of the available evidence. In 1696, for example, John Houghton[1] reported that there were three glassworks in Yorkshire but no others in the whole north and east of the country from Coventry to Newcastle. (It will be seen there were probably five – one in West Yorkshire and four in South Yorkshire at this time). Furthermore, by 1881 local glassworks had created a virtually world-wide monopoly in bottles for aerated waters and Matsumura (1983:Chapt.1) concludes from his analysis of the national industry that Yorkshire was then third in order of the number of glassworkers employed, having 16.7% of the national total.

It is perhaps a further reproach when it can be shown that twenty-five glassworks were operating in the region at the end of the nineteenth century and their socio-economic impact must have been considerable.

Reasons for this seeming indifference are not hard to find and part of the blame must lie with the region itself. The rapid development of deep mining in the eighteenth century generated by the country's insatiable demand for coal and the almost unassailable position of the Sheffield iron and steel industry in the international market overshadowed glassmaking as the region's third heavy industry. Glass was unable to compete successfully against coal and steel for investment capital to provide sustained growth for which an international market was essential, partly because of the crippling taxes on glassmaking between 1745 and 1845 and also because the area was originally land-locked making large scale exporting unrealistic in the early years.

These and other reasons for the later decline of the industry will be examined but the region has demonstrated its own indifference to a passing industry – if a glassworks failed, it was removed and the site occupied by a more profitable enterprise.

It is unfortunate for the history of the industry that in the early years of this century, when it was so much in decline, there was no interested local observer to record these rapid changes in its fortunes. Pioneering work by Francis Buckley (1925 and 1927), for example, firmly established a corpus of knowledge in areas such as Bristol and Stourbridge on which economic historians could build; no such base emerged for South Yorkshire. Buckley (1924:268) himself is almost apologetic in pointing out why this should be when he writes of the region in 1924; 'Local and private records of glass-making are either non-existent or not open to research'.

The situation has changed little since then. The majority of works which have long disappeared left no records whatsoever and the few documents to survive are sparse, forming no coherent story for any of the glassworks, valuable though they are in illuminating certain aspects. Recent archaeological research has, however, provided some further evidence in support of this fragmentary archive.

In view of these strictures the story must therefore be incomplete and this review can only present an outline of the role of the South Yorkshire glass industry in the light of current evidence. More detailed knowledge of its products and economics, capital structure and social organisation must await the emergence of, as yet, undiscovered archives and archaeological evidence.

It is convenient, though arbitrary, to divide the history of the South Yorkshire glass industry into sections by the centuries in which groups of glassworks were founded (Figure 1). Some degree of overlap is inevitable as many continued into succeeding centuries, often rebuilding with a revised technology, but these changes approximate to the century divisions as do the improvements in transport facilities in the region.

It should perhaps be noted that earlier documentary evidence always refers to 'glasshouses' but, as the modern use of the word causes some confusion with what is meant by a 'greenhouse' in horticulture, the term 'glassworks' is used here throughout except when making direct quotations from documents.

4

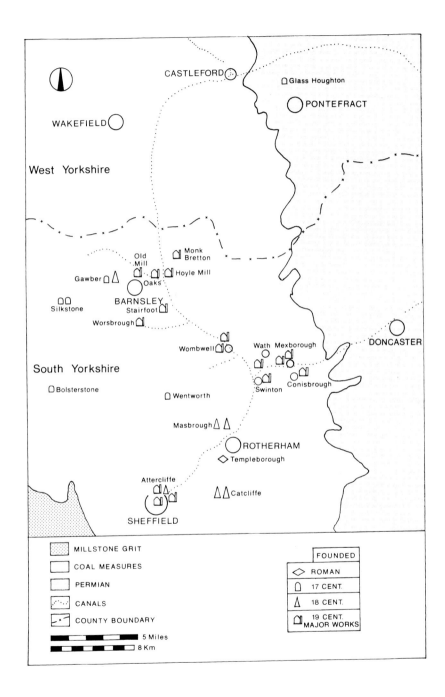

Figure 1   Distribution of South Yorkshire Glassworks

5

CHAPTER 1

NATIONAL HISTORICAL CONTEXT

ROMAN AND MEDIEVAL

Archaeological evidence points to glass having been made on a small scale during the Roman occupation of Britain (Hurst-Vose 1980:132–133) though it appears not to have survived into the fifth century and played no part in the establishment of the later British industry.

The evidence from South Yorkshire is typical of the period as seen from the excavations in 1916/17 at the first century Roman fort of Templeborough (known as 'Morbium' to the Romans), near Rotherham, which revealed fragments of glass bowls, beakers, small bottles etc. scattered over the site (May;1922). Some of this glassware had probably been made outside the east corner of the fort in a part of the civil settlement referred to by the excavators as the 'industrial annexe' where the remains of a building containing a small furnace and other evidence of a 'smithy' were found. However, also within the building were quantities of glass drips, runs and clippings which showed that clear soda glass had been worked at a possible second furnace. The material is preserved at the Clifton Park Museum, Rotherham, but no detailed drawings or photographs of the furnace site were made at the time. More positive evidence is unlikely as the area was later destroyed under a steelworks.

No further glass was produced in South Yorkshire until the seventeenth century.

The rest of Britain fared little better throughout the Anglo/Saxon and early medieval centuries and it was generally accepted even at the time that the relatively insignificant amounts produced were vastly inferior to the Continental imports (Charleston 1984:11–16).

An improving situation during the early post-medieval period has been shown by Crossley (1967:64–65) in his summation of the evidence obtained from excavations in Staffordshire at Abbots Bromley. During the sixteenth century an increasing domestic demand for window glass was to some extent being accommodated, particularly from the by then established industry in the Sussex Weald, but the supply of luxury and vessel glass still relied almost totally on imports (Godfrey 1975:10).

The political decision in 1567 granting glassmaking patents to the Antwerp glass merchant Jean Carré and the Venetian, Giacomo Verzelini, encouraging them to bring over Continental workers and set up glassworks in England, marks the true beginning of the British industry (Thorpe 1935:94; Godfrey 1975:16–28). It was intended that they 'teach the craft to native Englishmen' but the apparent insularity of the immigrants made this a slow process.

The group of immigrant Lorraine and Norman glassmakers originally associated with Carré was enlarged during the 1570s as the continuing persecution of Protestants on the continent led to further migrations. This was followed in turn by a movement away from the Weald through the Midlands and northward ultimately to Newcastle as the glassmakers sought cheaper fuel supplies for their wood-burning furnaces (Godfrey 1975:192).

South Yorkshire played no part in this sixteenth century expansion, partly because no wealthy landowner saw fit to risk his capital but partly because glassmaking was a wood-based fuel technology. Evidence suggests that the timber supplies in the region were already under pressure to the extent that by 1649 the report of the Parliamentary Surveyors at Barnsley saw 'noe wood within the mannor worth the valueing' (Hey 1979:131). Much of the standing timber in the area suitable for furnace use as charcoal was already earmarked for the thriving iron industry in the sixteenth century and tied into the furnace and forge operations such as those on the Earl of Shrewsbury's estates and the Rockley/Wortley ironworks (Crossley and Ashurst 1968:34–35; Raistrick 1938:51–86). A close relationship has been shown between managed woodland and an expanding iron industry in the Weald by Cleere and Crossley (1985:133–137) and there is evidence to suggest the situation was not dissimilar in South Yorkshire where woodlands continued to be managed for ironworking in the seventeenth and eighteenth centuries, for example, under the syndicate centred on the Spencer family at Cannon Hall, Barnsley (Andrews 1950). The migrant glassworker who required larger timber billets cut at a greater age than for charcoal would find little encouragement in the area.

Figures deduced by Crossley (1967:65) for glass production costs in Sussex point to two tons of wood billets being required to produce eight crowns of window glass – a 'crown' being a spun disc of glass up to a metre diameter. As transporting bulky fuel for even two or three miles could double its cost, it was more economic to rebuild a furnace in a new area when the local timber supply was exhausted. Although the case against the glassmakers regarding the depletion of the national resources of timber seems somewhat exaggerated, the alarms were, in general, no doubt well-founded. Godfrey (1975:50–54;191–192) in her analysis of the situation by the first decade of the seventeenth century and the effects on the economics of glassmaking as timber prices rose suggests that drastic measures to curb demands on timber were inevitable. In 1624 in Warwickshire, for example, the 'people rose in tumult, with curses and imprecations, and expelled the glassworkers' (Hartshorne 1887:174).

In 1615 a 'Proclamation touching Glass' was issued forbidding the burning of wood in the glass industry. Although some glassmakers continued to try to build wood-fired furnaces and were called before the Privy Council[1] the ban was totally effective within a few years.

MONOPOLIES

The proclamation should be seen, however, not in the light of a simple conservation matter but rather as part of the sequence of events to centralise the control of glass production.

> 'The government's policy to standardize and maintain quality was a constant quest throughout the reigns of Elizabeth, James and Charles' (Thirsk 1978:116).

This process was encouraged by the granting of monopoly patents by the Crown to those prepared to risk capital in various industries – alum, iron, soap etc. Such a patent was intended to give its owner total control over an industry, both production and distribution, in return for a payment to the Crown and played a crucial role in the developing glass industry.

Although constantly disputed and renewed throughout the early seventeenth century, the full glass patent was granted by James I to the courtier Sir Edward Zouch and partners in 1614 giving rights to produce all kinds of glass.[2] The patent covered the making of glass using coal fuel and all previous patents were withdrawn. It was renewed in 1615 but soon afterward Sir Robert Mansell bought out the Zouch partnership to become sole patentee controlling all glassmaking until the withdrawal of patents in 1642 (Godfrey 1975: 80–133). Mansell's monopoly was vigourously opposed by Isaac Bungar who was related by marriage to the original sixteenth century Lorraine immigrants (Charleston 1984:77). The system had never been universally popular and, although Bungar's opposition was not without self-interest, it represented a wider feeling. However, the convenience of the patents as a source of revenue was sufficient incentive for the Crown to brook any general opposition.

It can thus be seen that the period of Mansell's monopoly during the early years of the seventeenth century was the most significant in the history of glassmaking covering, as it does, the great technological changes brought about by the need to seek out a new fuel after the banning of wood and the changing role of the glassmaker himself. However, despite Dr. Godfreys extensive documentary research of the period and recent archaeological evidence, much remains to be understood.

The new coal furnaces were more expensive to build and the independent glassmaker who had to find his own markets might be seen in danger of being squeezed out in the new economic structure of the developing industry. Godfrey (1975:177) concludes that already 'a clear distinction between capital and labour had come about in the glass industry', though the conclusion may be a little premature. The evidence from South Yorkshire would suggest that the detail of the new technology was far from resolved and the independent glassmaker still thrived at the end of the century, having survived the Civil War and the rigours of the monopoly system. No doubt the monopolies encouraged a division of labour and capital but, at least during the second half of the seventeenth century, the freer market saw a brief return of the independent maker.

TECHNICAL CHANGE – WOOD TO COAL

It is generally agreed that the effects of the ban on timber were traumatic, far-reaching and permanent but must be judged ultimately as beneficial; in overcoming adversity the British glass industry was soon to be superior to that of the Continent, and admired as such, after centuries of being considered inferior (Charleston 1978:31–32). The great technological change enforced by the monopoly agreement had been forestalled to some extent, largely as a result of the rising timber costs early in the century which had encouraged attempts to use coal as an alternative fuel.

The invention of the coal-fired glass furnace has been credited to Thomas Percival about 1612 (Hartshorne 1887:182) some three years before the edict though he was, perhaps, merely claiming a formal patent for a design he had seen operating elsewhere. The situation remains confused with various other glassmakers such as Isaac Bungar also laying claim. Certainly by the second decade of the seventeenth century the technical problems had mainly been overcome and coal was being used successfully as shown by the results of excavations at Haughton Green near Manchester (Hurst-Vose 1980:143–146) and investigations at Sir William Clavell's glassworks at Kimmeridge in Dorset (Crossley 1987:340–382).

In essence the basic design change was simple. In wood-fired furnaces the wood billets were fed into the furnace along the ground into a trench created by the stone or clay banks at each side (sieges) on which stood the melting pots (crucibles), the whole being covered with a stone or clay dome (Figure 2A). The dome had access holes (gathering holes or bocca) through which the glassmaker passed his blowing iron or gathering rod to collect molten glass from the crucible. The flames made their exit through these holes which could be opened or closed using a stone slab to control the flow of air through the furnace; a method retained in all later furnaces.

Wood burns with a long flame and sufficient air was pulled through the flue at each end to generate the required temperature around the crucibles.

Coal, on the other hand, burns with a short flame and at too low a temperature unless air is forced through it. The vital feature of the coal-fired design is the iron grid onto which the coal was fed, (Figure 2B). Air flues constructed as deep trenches in the ground led under

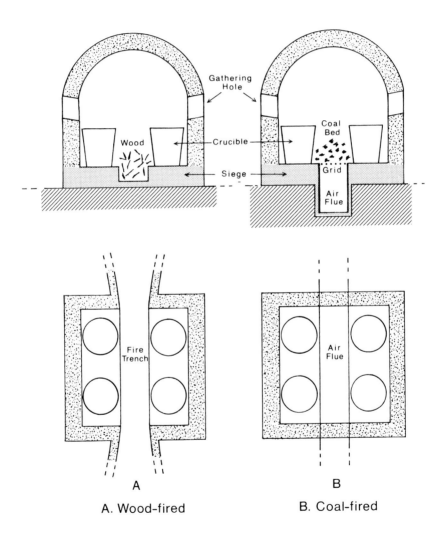

Figure 2   Glass Furnaces – Schematic

the grid so that incoming air passed through the burning coal to achieve the high temperature within the dome. The arrangement was often referred to as a 'wind furnace' and the principle of construction remained virtually unchanged into the twentieth century in all direct-fired furnaces.

CHAPTER 2

SOUTH YORKSHIRE ORIGINS

Under Mansell the industry began to expand away from the earlier centres such as the Weald (Thorpe 1935:89–90) to concentrate in areas where suitable cheap coal was readily available for the new furnaces, particularly to what became the traditional glassmaking areas around Stourbridge, Newcastle and Bristol. London exceptionally continued to be a centre of production in view of its attraction as a commercial focus and its capacity for cheap coastal and river transport whether requiring bulk timber or coal. Some glassworks such as at Newcastle were set up by Mansell himself, but his normal policy was to sub-let the right to operate a works.

This seventeenth century dispersal of the glass industry to the coalfields has traditionally been offered by local writers as the ready explanation for the arrival of glassmaking in South Yorkshire (McNair 1982). It is, however, too simplistic an interpretation of events and more akin to rationalisation after the event.

It cannot be disputed that the early decades of the seventeenth century witnessed the rapid development of the South Yorkshire coalfield, the wealthier landlords seeing potential for ready profit as, for example, the development of the mines on Barnsley Moor (Elliott 1988:140–150) and the area around Wentworth and Elsecar (Clayton 1966). Coal had become a popular source of fuel in the ever-expanding iron and steel industry of the region and population pressure from the growing towns and villages was reducing the available woods for domestic fuel, encouraging a change to coal. Even in the sixteenth century Leland had noted a local preference for coal as a domestic fuel:

> 'Though betwixt Cawoode and Rotherham be a good plenti of wood yet the people burne much yerth cole, by-cause hit is plentifully found ther, and sold good chepe. A mile from Rotherham be veri good pittes of cole. Halamshire hath plenti of woode, and yet ther is burnid much se cole' (Hey 1986:155).

By the seventeenth century coal was firmly established in the home.

Although shaft mining was not unknown, the predominant mining technique of the period was extraction by day-holes (drift mining), working into the edge of an outcrop. The west/east incline of the strata to the east of the Pennines created escarpments which are intersected by valleys to reveal bands of coal seams on the surface of hillsides which could be worked into under the hill. The method required little more than pick, shovel and tub demanding no outlay for machinery etc. Even timber for propping could be minimal; as the roof became unsafe the day-hole could simply be abandoned and a fresh start made nearby, resulting in a line of old crop workings such as can be found along the north side of the Little Don Valley near the Bolsterstone glassworks (Mitchell 1947:25).

The exploitation of the coalfield accelerated during the century on the secure base of industrial and domestic demand, offering clear attractions for the glassmaker needing easy access to suitable fuel supplies. Five coal-fired glassworks are now known to have existed in the area during the seventeenth century at Wentworth, Silkstone, Bolsterstone, Gawber I and at Glass Houghton suggesting that these attractions were recognised. It should be noted that the Report by John Houghton, referred to earlier, states there was 'one at Ferrybridge and two near Silkstone'. The first would be the one now known as Glass Houghton but it is not clear to which he refers as 'near Silkstone' particularly as there were two actually at Silkstone. He was, of course, reporting on those operating at the time of the 1696 survey and Wentworth had then closed but Bolsterstone and Gawber I are omitted. The five in Yorkshire compare nationally, for example, with Lancashire 2, Nottingham 4, Bristol 9 and Newcastle 11. (See Appendix A).

The glassmaker also needed refractory clay from which to make his crucibles and the local coal seams offered an excellent material in the associated ganister clay (Mitchell 1947:141). These clays were later exploited in the local potteries at Bolsterstone, Silkstone, Swinton, Rawmarsh and Mexborough.

The basic ingredient of glass is silica and, for the seventeenth century glassmaker, there were deposits of siliceous sandstone in the Coal Measure beds which, when weathered, produced a sand that was probably adequate for small scale production (Kenworthy 1918:9) or there were sand beds forming the Basal Permian sand on the western edges of the Permian rocks around Hampole and Bilham (Mitchell 1947:117).

The Magnesian Limestone of the Permian beds to the east of the region (Figure 1) had long been a source of building material and would supply the needs of the glassmakers for the lime (burnt limestone) as another major ingredient of glass.

It is clear that the region had much to offer the glassmaker seeking fresh fields; it is equally clear that many other areas were just as attractive and probably more accessible. It would, therefore, be a fair question to ask, why South Yorkshire?

The comments of Dr.Taylor (1983:12) on the inadequacies of the concept of geographical determinism in the location of settlements, apply equally to the location of industries:

'While there are clearly certain general physical determinants which cannot be ignored, for example a mining village can hardly grow up away from a coalfield ... most of the specific determinants of settlement location are probably not concerned with the physical nature of the site ...(which)... is of less importance in the decision to settle there than the human factor'.

The 'human factor' to which must be attributed the first glassworks marking the inception of the South Yorkshire glass industry was Thomas Wentworth, Chief Minister to King Charles I and created Earl of Strafford in 1640.

Figure 3   Glassblowing – Early 18th Century.

CHAPTER 3

17TH CENTURY FOUNDATIONS

HISTORY

By the mid-1620s Sir Robert Mansell theoretically had total control of the British glass industry through his monopoly patents, though his position was always uneasy and he felt constantly embattled. He regularly sought the support of the Earl of Strafford but correspondence between the two indicates that the Earl, like the King, had little interest in either glassmaking or Mansell's well-being; it was simply a matter of revenue. However, Mansell felt encouraged to increase the number of glassworks, particularly for the production of window glass and, in view of the Earl's position at Court and his extensive estates both in England and Ireland, he was an obvious candidate to be involved in this expansion. Mansell probably considered that Strafford's direct involvement with the industry through having his own glassworks would provide a safer haven of political strength to counter the continuing disaffection expressed toward the monopoly by Parliament. Correspondence between Mansell, Strafford and Richard Marris (Strafford's agent in the north) suggests the project was something less than Mansell's hopes.

However, in 1631, after insistant pressure from Marris, the Earl made available a small plot of land, now called Glasshouse Green, just beyond the estate wall of his mansion, Wentworth Woodhouse, a mile east of Wentworth village from which the family derived its name in the Middle Ages, between Barnsley and Sheffield. Some confusion has arisen from Hodkin (1953:21) trying to locate this glassworks by placing it in the '.. Gawber-Silkstone-Wentworth neighbourhood..' (when in fact there was one at each) and despite Joseph Hunter (1831:99) having named the site in the previous century.

The terms of the agreement appear to have been most unfavourable to Mansell, though perhaps not unusual for the times as Godfrey (1975:173) notes a comparable arrangement between Mansell and Sir Percival Willoughby at Wollaton in Staffordshire. Mansell was to pay all building costs at Wentworth, provide all raw materials, employ a glassmaker, arrange for marketing its products and pay rent to the Earl for the privilege of using the glassworks. In addition, he was to buy all the coal for the furnace from the Earl's Wentworth pits.

Clearly the Earl held the glass industry in low esteem as a possible source of personal profit and viewed the project with some caution;

> 'If either the commodity failed or Sir Robert [Mansell] die I lose my money, the profit I looke for being principally in the uttering of my Coles'.[1]

The glassworks was built solely for the production of window glass and Marris wrote to the Earl on 16 April 1632 that

> 'I have now at last finished the glass house which hath been a great trouble to me ... the next week they begin to make glass'.

According to Marris[2] it was a 'gudly great house coverd by the stone' costing £37 8s 4d together with '£89 and odd' for raw materials. Francis Bristow was put in as glassmaker in spite of his earlier clash with Mansell (Godfrey 1975:115) and he was to do his own marketing with the assistance of Marris, even though the Earl was reluctant to agree to this latter as he saw it as a waste of his agent's valued employment.

Analysis of samples found on the site (Appendix B) show the glass to have been a pale green/amber suitable for window glass but of dubious quality. A laboratory experimental batch prepared at the Department of Ceramics, Glasses and Polymers of Sheffield University using the same molecular proportions was reasonably stable. However, the analyses point to an excess of lime, which could lead to instability, and might indicate a measure of indifference by the Wentworth glassmaker towards his product.

No information on the market destination of the glass has been found but it may be relevant that the period coincided with the initial impetus of rebuilding houses in stone and the extensive adoption of glazed windows in the region as shown by Hey (1986:196–205) and

Giles (1986:106–109). The regional demand may yet be identified in this rebuilding phase.

The works, however, was destined for early closure. Mansell had over-reached himself financially in seeking an Irish monopoly, with Strafford's encouragement as Lord deputy of Ireland, and was seemingly physically tiring of the constant difficulties over his monopoly rights. The Earl of Strafford, of course, was having problems of his own concerning his association with the King and his role in the supposed threat of the rise of Catholicism. He was executed on Tower Hill in May 1641.

Further problems arose at the glassworks in 1642 when Mansell succeeded with a petition to the Lords for the imprisonment of Bristow for repeated non-payment of his monopoly dues. No reference to the glassworks can be found after this date and it is to be assumed Bristow's removal saw its closure. The actual site of the furnace has yet to be located.

The Wentworth glassworks must be viewed as an isolated brief excursion. A decade and a half elapsed before the next works was established in South Yorkshire, from when the story becomes continuous. A fine thread of continuity can be detected, however, through Bristow.

He provides an early example of the tendency to exclusivity amongst glassworkers – a tendancy which remained strong until the present century. Working with glass involves a high degree of manual dexterity using few tools, many improvised, and an almost innate sense of the behaviour of the material which, though almost infinitely malleable at its plastic working temperature, is virtually impossible to correct if the initial shaping falters. Composition and proportions of its raw materials were often guarded as family secrets.

This exclusiveness was no doubt encouraged among the sixteenth and seventeeth century immigrants with their problems of social integration not being helped by having been brought in as 'experts' in the first place. Local resentment would be natural.

Bristow, although British born, had married into the Bungar family, one of the familiar family groups of immigrants which are found at successive glassworks as the industry spread northward in the sixteenth and seventeenth centuries (Pape 1933). He had been working at the DeHowe glassworks at Haughton Green, near

Manchester, where another French family, Pilmay, was also working (Hurst-Vose 1980; Ashurst 1992).

The Pilmays first appear amongst the immigrants near Salisbury in 1599:

> John Pillney a Frenchman of the glasshouse buried[3]

Later they are in Eccleshall in Shropshire:

> 1608 Adam Pilmaye glassmaker buried 12 November[4]

In 1619 they had arrived at Haughton Green and were clearly rising in stature in the industry by marrying into the DeHow family who owned the glassworks:

> 1619/20 George Piline and Abygall Dehow married 22 January[5]

Of particular relevance is the parish register entry for the 7th of February 1634/35:

> John Pilme married Alice Dehow[6]

They had three children John, Peter and Mary but, from the Will of Alice Pilmay[7] in 1672, John the elder appears to have remarried another Alice, Widow Bullney, who already had a son John Bullney and grandchildren John and Benjamin. The Bullneys remained in Lancashire but the Pilmays crossed the Pennines to settle in the village of Silkstone, three miles west of Barnsley. The site of the glassworks is now marked on maps as the 'Pot House' but it had been noted in 1718 by John Warburton[8] when preparing his map of Yorkshire – 'Silkstone church ... pass a Rill at the Bottom. The Glass house on the Rt.'.

No doubt their move was occasioned by the destruction of the Haughton Green glassworks during a Civil War skirmish in 1653 (Hurst-Vose, 1980:146). But from the evidence in the Manchester Quarter Sessions records the locals may not have been too unhappy to see them go as not being the best of neighbours. Frequent entries refer to their 'not keeping the peace'. In Midsummer 1636, for example, John Pilmay was bound '.. to keep the peace to Llamas Grundye labourer' and his brother George Pilmay was also '.. to keep the peace to Llamas Grundye' in 1636 and again in 1636 to Ragliffe (yeoman) and a Wragley.

The site they chose near the mill in Silkstone was owned by William Scott of a prosperous yeoman family and, when he died in 1655, John Pilmay junior married his widow Abigail on 26 September 1658. The business prospered and their local standing rose; John is later referred to by the title 'Mr' whilst his sister Mary married John Moore of a local family. Peter remained unmarried. Even so, their initial introduction to South Yorkshire society was perhaps not as smooth as they may have wished as the Rotherham Quarter Sessions for 19 July 1664 records: John Pillmay, glassmaker, Silkstone assaulted by Hugo Shearburne.

Abigail Pilmay's Will and Probate Inventory survive[9] which show there were two furnaces operating, one producing common bottle and window glass, the other fine quality lead (white) glass for tableware. She had ashes from burnt vegetation (rape) worth £20 which provided the alkali, red lead, Breeley sand and 'blew powder' (presumably a cobalt compound for coloured glasses). There were various moulds, blowing irons and even 'Fretting clay' for crucibles.

The documents also illustrate what was a 'normal way of life' in the villages and hamlets of the coal measures by 'combining agriculture with a craft' (Hey 1986:149). Farming was still, perhaps, the dominant occupation in the Pilmay/Scott arrangement but

> 'It was the rule rather than the exception for craftsmen to have a
> land holding that provided food for the family, and perhaps even
> a small surplus to sell' (Thirsk 1978:110).

Together with the slightly later, 1707, Inventory of her son John Scott (by her first marriage)[10] it is clear that farming took precedence. Abigail had:

> 'corne, Straw..in the barn £6, one hay Stack £1 15s 0d, one mare,
> Saddle & Girth, 2 Cows, 2 heaffers & 1 Steer £11 10s 0d, Two
> swine £1 8s 0d.'

John Scott had:

> '..in the dineing room: 10 loads of wheat 4s, 2 loads of peas 8s.
> In the Chamber over the dineing room: 5 quarter malt £5 7s 6d,
> abt. 4 stone of wool .. 4 wheels . In the barn: sixteen Loads of
> Wheat at 8s p. Load £6 8s 0d, a parcell of hay and Straw £2.'

He also had two hay stacks, manure, two carts, two waines, two harrows, 4 oxen, 3 cows, 3 mares, two geldings and a flock of sheep on the Coale Pitt hill in addition to '..a wheel barrow, Gavelock, hack, three picks and coale pit roapes.'

They lived well enough, however, to have plenty of linen, table cloths, knives, mirrors and upholstered chairs and stools which were far from common in the late 17th century.

Clearly the itinerant 'professional' glassmaker of the seventeenth century such as Bristow may have felt secure in following his trade as either employee or partner but the small independent glassmaker felt it prudent to find support for his independence in agriculture. The Wakefield Court Rolls of the time even show an unnamed Silkstone glassworker failed to appear before the court because 'he was at plow'.

Abigail carried on the works after the deaths of John (1675) and Peter (1697), even petitioning Parliament against the Glass Tax in 1696. On her death in 1698 it passed to John Scott, son by her first marriage. His Inventory of 1707 shows that one glassworks building had become a kitchen but the other still produced flint glass. However, the Inventory of his son, also called John[11] taken in 1747 makes no mention of a glassworks and a mortgage[12] of 1748 merely refers to '.. land adjacent to the old glasshouse'.

Glassmaking at Silkstone had ceased by then and, as a not uncommon sequel with old glassworks, the site developed into a pottery even though this meant building new furnaces as a glass furnace could not be used to fire pottery. The development is understandable, however, in view of the ready coal supply and availability of a suitable clay which the potters had previously used to make crucibles. A Deed (lease & release)[13] made between James Scott to John Richardson and Henry Wagstaffe in 1754 includes '.. pot ovens..' but no mention of the glassworks. An 1810 sketch by J.C. Nattes in the Cannon Hall Museum, Cawthorne, illustrates the pot kilns. Work is currently in progress to locate the actual glass furnace sites.

The parish registers show that John Townend and Ephraim Burdett were two of the glassmakers working with the Pilmays at Silkstone. A third was Francis Morton who married Abigail's grand-daughter, Mary Scott, and is to be found working at later glassworks such as Bolsterstone and Gawber (Kenworthy 1918:7). Morton's descendants form a long line of glassmakers working well into the nineteenth century at glassworks in the present West Yorkshire area around Castleford and Rothwell.

The first glassworks in the series which eventually formed that West Yorkshire industry was the one which John Houghton had called 'Ferrybridge' in 1696. It is now identifed as being in the village of Houghton, later absorbed within Castleford (Figure 1) and renamed Glass Houghton in 1756 (Goodchild 1970). It is included here as being the only other glassworks in the whole of Yorkshire in the seventeenth century, though it does have a connection with the South Yorkshire industry in that William Clifton, its owner, joined Abigail Pilmay and bottle makers from Lynn in Norfolk when petitioning Parliament against the 1696 glass tax. The works existed from at least 1691 to the mid-1740s (Figure 4) and was the only Yorkshire glassworks visited by that intrepid traveller, Celia Fiennes. She described:

> 'A Glass House – we saw them blowing white glass and neale in a large oven by the heat of the furnace; all the country is full of coal and pitts are so thick in the road that it is hazardous to travel for strangers.'(Morris 1947:94)

Returning to South Yorkshire, a minor works which has only been identified from archaeological evidence was found at the village of Gawber, between Barnsley and Silkstone. Referred to here as Gawber I, it was discovered during the excavations of the later, eighteenth century, glassworks site which is referred to as Gawber II (see Figure 15). It was a simple coal-fired furnace which had been largely destroyed in building the later works and could be dated only by thermo-remanent magnetic evidence to a last firing about 1700–1710 though its previous length of service cannot be known. Finds indicated it had produced lead glass (Ashurst 1970:101–103).

The remaining seventeenth century South Yorkshire glassworks was at Stocksbridge. It is, however, usually referred to as the Bolsterstone works because its site at Bate Green was in Bolsterstone parish and the town of Stocksbridge did not then exist. As in the case of Silkstone, modern maps name it as the 'Pot House'. It was operated by the Fox family, originally from Fulwood Hall in Sheffield, from its foundation in the 1650s until its closure in 1758. George Fox, nephew of the founder John Fox, married Mary Pole in 1679 who then

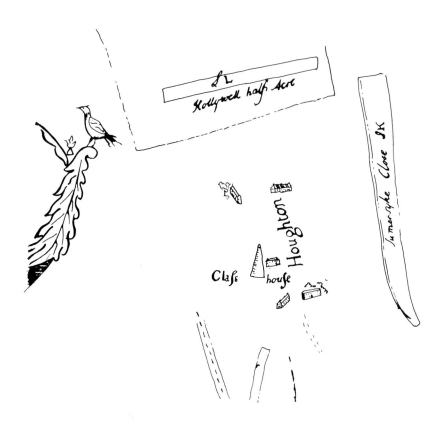

Figure 4   Glass Houghton – 18th century estate plan.

married Robert Blackburn in 1702 following the death of George in 1692 (Ashurst 1987:149–150). After Blackburn's death in 1727 John Fox (son of George and Mary) ran the works in addition to a pottery at the Sheffield Manor[14]. On his death in 1738 Mary took over and, in her Will of 1738, left it to her grandson Michael who died in 1758. With his death the Bolsterstone works closed for various reasons to be discussed later, but excavations in the 1980s have shown that, during its lifetime, it was one of the leaders in the new coal furnace technology and worthy of greater recognition. The superstructure of the glass melting furnace was destroyed after closure and the building converted to farm use. A pottery was established nearby, making earthenware with slip decoration in the style of the Midhope potters, from 1778 to the end of the eighteenth century (Ashurst 1987:204–206).

It is unlikely the Fox family were actual glassmakers, rather they were entrepreneurs who employed skilled men brought in from elsewhere. There is no evidence of French immigrant families working at Bolsterstone as there is for Silkstone but Richard Dixon, who had come from Worcester to manage Bolsterstone in the late seventeenth century, was related by marriage to the Henzeys, glassmakers from Lorraine who had founded the seventeenth century Newcastle glass industry. He left in 1702 to found his own works at Whittington and the Sitwell family papers at Renishaw contain records of glass bought from Whittington suggesting Dixon may well have been a supplier when at Bolsterstone.

Near the time of the works' closure the manager was called Swinden and it is significant that members of the Swinden family are found at glassworks throughout both South and West Yorkshire late into the nineteenth century. This tendency amongst glassworkers to pass on their skills within the family to keep their secrets is even better exemplified in the case of William Fenney who was managing the works in the early eighteenth century.

The origins of the Fenney family are obscure but their influence in the glass industry was widespread: in the 1720s Henry Fenney was running Glass Houghton, Joshua Fenney at Rothwell Hague and other Fenneys are found at Thatto Heath and Eccleston in Lancashire.

The possibilities open to such craftsmen are summarised by Sidney and Beatrice Webb (1920:6) with perhaps a hint of cynicism that,

'So long as industry was carried on mainly by small masters, each employing but one or two journeymen .. the industrious apprentice might reasonably hope, if not always to marry his master's daughter, at least hope to set up in business for himself.'

William Fenney did both. In I718 he married Mary Fox, the owner's daughter, but in 1738 a dispute arose at Bolsterstone when Fenney clearly wished to expand and build a works incorporating the new technology. His mother-in-law Mary Blackburn, who was now a widow again after the death of Robert Blackburn in 1727, clearly wished everything to remain as it was. In her Will[15] she forbids Fenney to

'.. set up or carry on a Gain in Partnership with or have any concern or employment in any other Glasshouse whatsoever within the distance of ten computed miles from my said glasshouse at Bate Green'.

The dispute was not settled and Mary added a codicil to her Will[16] by letter to her executors:

'.. whereas my son in law William Fene has given mee such aprehncion of beeing troublesum by his design of setting up a Glashous at boulster stone made me allter my will for I would loath have it that what I leav should bee the caus of breach of charity soe I have alltred my will that if Will:fene does prove letigous his children shall loos what I have left them in my will but if he will give my executors such securitys as the aprove that hee will not set up or ioyn within ten miles of this place the pore children shall have there legacys..'

He gave up the struggle and moved to Catcliffe, between Sheffield and Rotherham, where Joseph Hunter (1831:35) notes

'A glasshouse was established in 1740, by a company of persons who had been previously employed in the glasshouse near Bolsterstone, then in high reputation.'

In making the move Fenney founded the next wave of glassworks in the region to be reviewed in Chapter 4 concerning the eighteenth century consolidation of the South Yorkshire industry.

TECHNOLOGY

Furnace

Urban landscape historians could be forgiven for asking how a seventeenth century glassworks might be recognised. This does, of course, beg the question that there is such a thing as a 'typical' seventeenth century glassworks to recognise and current evidence, small as it is, would suggest otherwise. For the early years of the century, the Haughton Green excavations can offer no evidence of the building which enclosed the furnace and Crossley (1987:354) hesitantly postulates a timber frame on insubstantial stone footings at Kimmeridge. With equal hesitancy a timber building with tile roof is suggested for the early Gawber I furnace (Ashurst 1986:354). Such buildings are unlikely to survive in any location.

The later stone buildings in centres such as Newcastle, Stourbridge or London have been at even greater risk, being situated in urban areas subjected to repeated industrial development. In South Yorkshire, however, it might be hoped that as the seventeenth century glassworks were set up in rural areas on the periphery of the coalfield to take advantage of the coal outcrops – areas not affected by later industrialisation – survival might be possible. The hope is partially realised but the evidence offers little by way of definition of a 'glassworks' in the way that, perhaps, a 'laithe house' or 'field barn' might be instantly recognisable to the landscape historian.

The earliest Gawber furnace was destroyed by a later works; a Methodist chapel was built over the Glass Houghton site; Wentworth was known to be built of 'gudly stone' but later farm buildings have obscured whatever original building may survive; much of Silkstone was cleared in 1964 when a garden centre was established though a seventeenth century building with an arched entrance is being investigated as a likely site.

Only at Bolsterstone has it been possible to confirm a standing building associated with a dated glass furnace (Ashurst 1987: 155–173). Large open arches on both side walls are a prominent feature with the deep airway leading to the furnace within the building (Figure 5). The archaeological survey shows the remains of the original walls of the glassworks. The open arches had been blocked

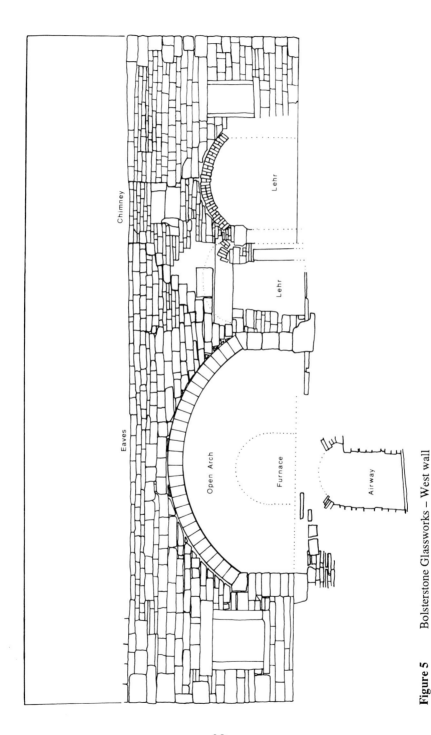

Figure 5   Bolsterstone Glassworks – West wall

when converted to a farm building but were intended to be open as drawn. Two smaller brick arches on the west wall are the remains of the lehrs which had unfortunately partly collapsed.

The lehrs, or annealing chambers, were an essential part of the glassmaking process where the finished articles were reheated then allowed to cool slowly over many days to remove all stress from the glass. Without this annealing the object would immediately shatter in use. At Bolsterstone one lehr could be cooling whilst the other was being filled but an alternative system was to use a single long tunnel as at the eighteenth century Redhouse works near Dudley, Staffordshire. The tunnel was hot at one end, cool at the other, and the articles were moved slowly along it.

Excavations in the 1980s (Ashurst 1987:147–226) found the technology of the actual melting furnace at Bolsterstone to be totally unlike expectations for the period. The review of early glass furnace technology by Charleston (1978) would suggest the later seventeenth century furnace to have a simple, straight through, underground airway leading to the coal grid. Bolsterstone had four. A major drawback of the direct furnace was the loss of heat as fresh cold air passed through the coal and a further innovation found at Bolsterstone was provision for pre-heating the incoming air. This regenerative process was not found even in the next series of eighteenth century furnaces and was only widely adopted in the later nineteenth century.

Lumps of coal were fed into the furnace from each end onto the central grid between the sieges and ultimately around the pots. The heat rising through the gathering holes and vents pulled in air from the airways through the coal. It can be seen from the reconstruction drawing (Figure 6) that air rising through the furnace was compressed by the narrowing of the furnace walls and some of the heated air within the dome was fed back into the lower air intake to pre-heat the fresh air. Such a system has proved to be highly efficient. The normal direct furnace of the period would require nine tons of coal to produce a ton of glass but at least two tons could be saved by such pre-heating.

Such a saving is particularly important when it is remembered that the furnace never went out throughout its working life which could be many months or even years. The whole structure, dome and all, were maintained at red heat, even at night or week-end when the gathering holes were closed to conserve fuel, as the glass in the crucibles had to remain molten ready for the next working day.

31

Figure 6   Bolsterstone Glassworks – Furnace reconstruction.

A vital job in all glassworks at the end of each day was the removal of clinker from the grid by the 'teaser' who walked down the airway and, standing under the furnace at its full heat in excess of 1000° C, had to prise it out with an iron bar. Bars were fixed across the furnace walls below the sieges to provide leverage for his teaser bar. Clinker and ash were then shovelled into a barrow and wheeled to the end of an airway to be removed. Though covered in water-soaked sacking before entering the heart of the furnace, this must be classed as the least desirable of occupations!

Almost as difficult was the changing of a crucible in a glass furnace when it was worn out or a different glass mix was required. Part of the front wall had to be removed with the furnace still working at full white heat and the crucible removed using iron bars. The new crucible, already glowing red-hot from preheating in another furnace, had to be manoeuvered into its position on the siege although it could weigh around six or seven hundredweights when full of glass. The wall had then to be rebuilt by the furnaceman, again covered with soaked sacking, dashing up to the furnace, replacing perhaps a couple of stones at a time set in clay, until the wall and gathering holes were replaced.

If the crucible maker had failed to do his job properly the result could be even more dramatic should a crucible burst within the furnace. Molten glass would pour out over the sieges and coal bed making the furnace unusable. This would be a disaster for the glassworks owner as it would normally enforce a complete renewal of the furnace, but the heavy stonework for some feet around the furnace would be at red heat and need a considerable time to cool sufficiently to undertake such rebuilding. Many days or weeks of production would be lost. Archaeological evidence at Bolsterstone indicated that this had indeed happened with a crucible containing blue glass and may have partly influenced the decision to close the works.

Crucibles

The crucibles in which the glass was melted were made from ganister clay with a percentage of grog and a tested sample from Gawber showed a composition of: Clay particle size less than 0.13mm = 79%

Grog size 2mm to 7mm = 12% Fine sand = 8.7 %. The sample was test-fired to a temperature in excess of 1250° C and a 60mm x 5mm sample could not be broken by hand, illustrating its strength (Ashurst 1970:138).

The clay had to be trod with bare feet for many hours or even days to ensure that all air had been excluded otherwise the tiny air bubbles could explode in the heat of the furnace and shatter the crucible. A new crucible was heated, slowly at first, in a secondary furnace for two or three days to bring it to red heat (soaking) before being introduced to the main melting furnace. As the glass was used up, fresh raw materials could be added through the gathering hole. Crucibles could normally be expected to last three to four months, and exceptionally even six. But it was not unknown, at least in the seventeenth century, for the potters to ensure their continued employment by deliberately sabotaging the crucibles so that they fractured during soaking ensuring a steady demand for their services. When Sir Robert Mansell was setting up his Newcastle enterprise he purchased his pot clay from Staffordshire and brought a case against some suppliers as

> '... some of the petitioners caused its corruption, with the result that the pots broke'.

He then sent to Rouen, in France, for his clay but his problems were not over as this

> '... was also spoilt, in all probability by the procurement of Bongar through his kinsmen there'.

Various types had evolved over the centuries, tubular, barrel and 'plantpot' shape but the latter had become the standard English crucible by the seventeenth century (Figure 7).

Usually referred to as an 'open pot' it had proved ideal over the centuries for all types of glass made in a wood-fired furnace but, on the change to coal, a major problem arose. The glass was exposed to the atmosphere within the furnace and Diderot (1765:107) complains that

> '.. particles of coal would keep falling on the glass, making it reboil, and the bubbles or blisters produced in this way would spoil the products..'

30
c m

Figure 7   Open crucible

30
c m

Figure 8   Closed crucible

A more serious problem, however, was the effect of the fumes from the coal, particularly those derived from the sulphur content. These could discolour the glass to give a smokey green, or brown to even black glass. This mattered little when making common wine bottles but was disastrous if trying to make a clear or a delicately coloured glass, especially if it was a lead crystal glass.

The solution was the invention of a 'closed pot' (Figure 8). This is usually attributed to Thomas Percival between 1611–1614 which

> '...marks an epoch in the history of glassmaking, resulting eventually in the manufacture in England of the most brilliant crystal glass ever produced in the world' (Hartshorne 1887).

This may, however, be merely formal recognition of a patent for a practice already followed by glassmen. Archaeological evidence from Haughton Green suggests early trials had seen the use of a lid with a side hole in the pot to allow access to the glass but, as there are no descriptions or drawings of a completely closed pot of this early period, its design was completely unknown until the 1980s excavations at Bolsterstone.

Upwards of half a ton of crucible fragments were found amongst which were some which clearly did not form part of the standard 'plantpot' shape. Painstaking restoration work of the scattered fragments has made it possible to partially reassemble three crucibles which represent the only known examples of the seventeenth /eighteenth century closed crucible.

The dome prevented ingress of any furnace atmosphere to the molten glass and the mouth would be fitted close to the gathering hole to allow access for the glassmakers blowing iron but exclude fumes. Built up using one inch thick coils of clay they had a capacity of 19 gallons providing approximately 4 cwt of molten glass. One example had a hole in its top which might appear to conflict with the principle of keeping out the furnace fumes. This is explained, however, by the practicalities of using closed crucibles. In an open pot the furnace flames could reach the glass surface itself and a few hours could be sufficient to melt up a new batch but with a closed crucible only the pot itself is directly heated and melting could take up to three days. When a new type of glass was required urgently, the seventeenth century glassmakers realised that by making a small hole in the top this heating up time could be reduced to twelve hours at small risk to the contents.

This design of crucible for use in coal furnaces was so successful that it has never been improved. It was not only used throughout the entire glass industry until the end of the nineteenth century when a new technology replaced it for mass production, but is still in use today at factories producing hand-made glassware.

PRODUCTS AND MARKETS

All the early South Yorkshire glassworks produced window glass, in fact Wentworth was built for no other purpose. It was made in the traditional 'crown' glass method of the Lorrainer immigrants (as opposed to the alternative cylinder method of the Normandy immigrants). Glass was gathered on the blowing iron and blown into a bubble. This was then punctured and, keeping it malleable using the flames from the gathering hole or a separate furnace, was spun out into a disc about two to three feet diameter after being transferred to the pontil – an iron bar about eight feet long. After annealing, the outer part was cut into small squares or diamonds leaving the centre as waste. Now often referred to as a 'bulls eye', this centre was in fact rarely used, being too thick to cut and usually impure. It is a mistaken modern fashion to incorporate artificial ones in windows hoping to create an 'olde Englande' effect.

The increased demand for window glass had been created by the considerable rebuilding and refurbishing of houses and churches taking place in the region. Unfortunately few records of actual sales survive. In 1727 the Earl of Strafford was charged by Robert Blackburn of Bolsterstone '... for the glass for Barnsley church windows...' (Wilkinson 1870:401) and in his Probate Inventory of that year Blackburn held window glass worth £40 in store. The Inventory also comments on £20 of goods in the 'chapmans store' indicating that the goods were purchased by chapmen (travelling salesmen), probably on credit, which they would carry around the country on back packs or by horse if successful enough (Hey 1980).

He also held bottles worth £25 which were the other staple of the glass industry. Until the early years of the century, wines and beers had been served at table in stone bottles but the new fashion of serving it in glass bottles filled from a barrel in the cellar created a heavy national demand. The Silkstone and Bolsterstone glassworks began to supply that demand and the South Yorkshire industry has continued to do so to the present day. The seventeenth century design was a simple globe, easily blown without use of a mould, but with the bottom pushed inward as an 'upkick' to provide stability. A strip of glass called the 'string rim, was wound round the neck, just below the lip, to which the wooden stopper could be wired. No complete examples survive from Bolsterstone but an interesting sample of Silkstone ware is preserved at the Village Museum in Cawthorne, near Barnsley.

Window glass and bottles were made from the common sand/alkali/lime mix as were the occasional specialist items such as those ordered by the Earl of Strafford when his gardener wished to adopt the latest ideas in horticulture by growing young plants under glass. In 1719 his Steward asked

> '... if your lordship would be pleased to let me have 2 dozen of bell glasses which I can have them made at Mr Blackborns at Boulsterstone..'[17]

However, the archaeological evidence at the early Gawber furnace and the Probate Inventories of both Abigail Pilmay at Silkstone and Robert Blackburn at Bolsterstone include red lead showing that lead crystal glass was made at these works. By the end of the century wine glasses had reached a high level of artistry and, whilst a number made at the Bolsterstone works have survived in private collections and in the Sheffield University Museum, the only evidence from Silkstone is a note for November 1659 in the Memorandum book of Henry Power of New Hall in Elland, near Huddersfield, that he

> '...pays John Wilson his man 2s vid for fetching glasses from the glasse house at Silkstone'[18]

With its advanced furnace design and extensive use of closed crucibles it was possible for Bolsterstone to produce some of the finest glass to rival any glassworks of the period.

Archaeological evidence showed it produced a wide variety of household glass incorporating a range of colours including amber, red, green, mauve and particularly deep blue.

Figure 9   17th century glass bottle

In addition a white enamel was made which contained a surprising 52.8% of lead oxide (See Analysis, Appendix B). Though added to some articles in the form of decorative strips its main use was in conjunction with a deep brown, almost black, glass in producing bottles, jars, flasks etc. in a style of glassware known as 'Nailsea' glass (Figure 10). A gather of the dark glass was rolled in enamel chippings then blown to shape. During the process the enamel expanded to form characteristic white blotches and streaks on the dark background.

It must be added that the Nailsea works, near Bristol, after which this style is named, did not come into production until 1788 and originally only made common bottles. The Bolsterstone works was producing this form of decorative glass before it closed about 1758 and the question must be raised as to the discrepancy of date and name. No positive answer can be given but local opinion suspects that as chapmen took Bolsterstone glass to wider markets, particularly London, it would sell at a better price if purported to be a product of places such as Bristol with a centuries old tradition of glassmaking begun by the Tudor immigrants, than a new industry in the wilds of the north. Whatever the reason, collectors now refer to 'Nailsea type' glassware as it is clear the style has a long pedigree and could even have originated at Bolsterstone.

In the main, however, the seventeenth century South Yorkshire industry was concerned to supply everyday items such as bottles, inkwells, light fittings, cheap colourful jugs – even bird feeders. It was the kind of rural industry which Thirsk (1978:118) describes as

> '... flourishing quietly and without ostentation. They had a steadily loyal clientele because they offered a lot of serviceable goods – nothing expensive, just everyday necessities, plus some fancy wares that were cheap and cheerful, and came within the purses of working men and women'.

Unfortunately this was not enough to ensure the survival of the local industry without radical rebuilding and adoption of a new technology. The first phase of the South Yorkshire industry had run its course and so had its founders.

Wentworth closed ingloriously in 1641, the first Gawber furnace had ceased shortly after 1700, Silkstone struggled on after Abigail's death until perhaps the 1720s, Bolsterstone closed with the death of

Figure 10   Nailsea glass – Bolsterstone Glassworks

Figure 11   18th century Bolsterstone Glass.

Michael Fox in 1758. In addition to the lack of investment in the newer technology (as shown by Fenney's disagreement with his mother-in-law) and the absence of a new generation willing to continue the enterprise, both Silkstone and Bolsterstone suffered from transport problems in their somewhat isolated position. In the case of Bolsterstone its ability to produce a wide range of glasses was perhaps part of its own undoing. It lacked a mass product for a mass regional market to rival the new eighteenth century works which were being built, yet lacked adequate transport facilities to reach distant markets with its quality products. The introduction of the 1745 Glass Tax, discussed in the next chapter, was probably the last straw to a struggling works.

The new eighteenth century glass technology demanded even greater supplies of coal and South Yorkshire had it in abundance, but not in the areas chosen by the original founders and the industry made its first move eastward to where the new deep mines were exploiting richer veins.

CHAPTER 4

18TH CENTURY CONSOLIDATION

HISTORY

The seventeenth century may have been characterised by a total lack of conformity in the construction of glassworks buildings as the glassmakers wrestled with the technical problems of using coal fuel but, in contrast, the eighteenth century English glassworks is to be instantly recognised by its high brick cone which enclosed the entire furnace and its working area. Large doorways punctuate the base and the apex is left open as a small chimney approximately a metre wide. Its distinctive straight-sided conical shape differentiates it from the 'bottle-shaped' pottery kilns and cementation furnaces also developed during the period (Figure 12).

Its invention revolutionised glass production by increasing output and economy and must be seen as the single most important advance at the time which placed Britain finally amongst the leaders in the international field of glass production.

Some doubt still exists as to its origins but Charleston (1978:32) suggests it was perfected at the end of the seventeenth century, citing a Dublin example of 1696 and a 28.6m high cone in London by 1702. Well in excess of a hundred such cones must have been built in Britain during the century but only four now survive, in varying states of preservation:

Lemington, Newcastle on Tyne (36.6 m) built 1789.
Alloa Glass Works, Clackmannon, (27.4 m) rebuilt 1824.
Redhouse cone (30.5 m) at Stuart Crystal, Wordsley,
    Stourbridge built c.1790.
Catcliffe, near Sheffield (18.3 m) built c.1740.

Of these, only the Redhouse cone is sufficiently complete with airways and lehrs to convey a true impression of the advance in technology that the cone furnace represented.

Figure 12   Catcliffe Glassworks Cone

An early example, however, had stood at Gawber two miles north-west of Barnsley, built over the site of the abandoned seventeenth century furnace referred to previously. Nothing survived above ground as the brick cone had been removed in 1824 and soil imported over the field to convert it to arable land but excavations in 1968 (Ashurst, 1970:92–140) revealed the internal structure of a traditional English glass furnace of the early eighteenth century.

The works had been built by William Thorpe, a grocer from Glass Houghton, in 1732/3 on land leased from the Sitwells of Renishaw, Derbyshire, which included the nearby Gawber Hall, a sixteenth century timber-framed house.

Thorpe's venture into glassmaking immediately draws attention to the most dramatic change to affect the organisaion of the industry as such works demanded a considerable capital outlay, which the itinerant glassmaker or the part-time subsistence workers of an earlier age could not command. Owners and glassmakers were becoming divorced, laying the foundations for the later labour problems which bedevilled the industry. Thorpe was no glassmaker, though he would have been familiar with William Clifton's operation at Glass Houghton and clearly saw the chance for investment in an expanding industry.

Possibly being influenced by local knowledge of the earlier glass furnace, Thorpe selected his site on the Gawber outcrop of the eight foot seam of the 'Barnsley Coal' which he mined by a day-hole within a hundred yards of his cone. However, the mining operation was so successful (and the glass so troublesome as will be seen later) that the family changed their allegience from glass to coal and, having taken leases on numerous mines in the area, they relinquished the glassworks lease and it was up for sale in 1824. It was not sold as a going concern and the cone was demolished though some of the outbuildings and workshops survived until the 1930s. The mine continued in production under various changes of ownership until the 1940s.

The Darton Parish Registers show twenty-two families involved as glassmakers during the life of the works but, apart from the Mortons of Silkstone and the Glaisbrooks from Stourbridge, the origins of the remainder are obscure. Their destinations after closure have also yet to be determined, except for the Jephson family which co-founded the works at Whitwood Mere in West Yorkshire.

By the mid-eighteenth century the owner of the Glass Houghton works was less fortunate in his fuel supply. The coal reserves would have been adequate for the earlier works but its conversion to a cone led to its demise. A visitor in 1750 had commented

> '.. in the hill above the town there were formerly great coal works
> and a glass house; but the coal failing, the glass manufacture was
> discontinued' (Goodchild 1970).

(It has been noted by Matsumura (1983:14) that a similar failure overtook some of the Bristol glassworks as their coal supplies proved unequal to the demands of the new furnaces). The works was being used as a blacksmith's shop in 1839 but was demolished in 1846 and a Weslyan chapel built on the site.

Herbert Fenney had been involved at Glass Houghton and a relative, Joshua Fenney, operated a glassworks at Rothwell Hague, near Leeds. From this developed the West Yorkshire glass industry which, for the next two hundred years, ran parallel to, and rival to, the South Yorkshire industry until its closure this century. Its progress has been briefly outlined by Hodkin (1953) but a detailed history has yet to be written.

Following William Fenney's enforced move from Bolsterstone in 1740, he set up the Catcliffe works. Two cone furnaces were built, one of which still stands, preserved as an ancient monument open to the public, though unfortunately only the brick cone survives, its interior being concreted over for safety. A partial excavation by Sheffield City Museum in 1962 found little of its internal furnace arrangements but they were no doubt equivalent to those found at Gawber, to be described later.

Fenney's source of capital is unknown but the situation illustrates the two approaches which prevailed throughout the South Yorkshire involvement with glass. New works were set up either by entrepreneurs such as Thorpe whose knowledge of glass was minimal, regarding it simply as a profitable return on capital, or by ambitious skilled glass technicians who could obtain capital by taking in business partners or borrowing. Fenney was clearly the latter but, like many others, bankrupcy for such men was never far away as can be seen from the evidence Buckley found in the Midlands (Buckley:1927). Fenney probably under-estimated his capital needs and in 1759 the works was taken over by the relatively wealthy family of May who were followed by a partnership of Blunn & Booth from 1833. Henry Booth was an iron and steel magnate and Thomas Blunn had been described as a 'glass blower' when appointed a trustee of the Unitarian Old Meeting House, Rotherham – his family are to be found extending their glass interests into the nineteenth century. The Catcliffe works was the responsibility of Samuel Blunn in 1856 and his family last operated it as Blunn Brothers until its closure in 1884. A Trade Directory entry of 1901 suggests a brief revival by C. Wilcocks & Co. but this was a final, unsuccessful, fling.

At Masbrough, near Rotherham, John Wright and three friends pooled their resources in 1751 to build a glassworks beside the canal on land belonging to the Earl of Effingham. They were to pay £145

> '.. on account of the Building of the Glasshouse..' together with a total of £15 15s 0d for ' ... digging and casting up clay and making bricks at the glasshouse .'[1]

The cone they built was the first of a succession on the site, the last of which was demolished in 1945.

It would appear that, like Fenney, they too were under-capitalised and sought a new partner with fresh capital by advertising in the Newcastle Chronicle of 5th May 1769 to sell

> '... ten sixteenths of a Glasshouse .... the said glasshouse is contiguous to the River Don and well supplied with coals.'

The siting of this works illustrates the eighteenth century drift eastward into the now established deep mining area where coal supply was cheap and plentiful and where industry was also being influenced by the growing waterway network of the region as rivers were made navigable and canals developed.

The appeal, however, produced no new partner and, again in the Newcastle Chronicle, a further advertisement appeared on 10 May 1783:

> 'To be let ... two glasshouses at Rotherham. The one is a Crown House and the other a Bottle and Flint House. There is no other Crown House within 70 miles...'

(This last was a touch of advertising licence as the Gawber works fifteen miles away was also producing crown window glass).

John Beatson of Emley, landowner and businessman, bought the glassworks for his son William who took it over in June 1783 trading as W.Beatson & Co. In 1828 William's daughter married John Graves Clark of Hull and from their union originates the name of Beatson Clark under which the company now trades and which remained a family concern until its sale in 1988.

However, during that time the trading name repeatedly changed and trying to trace its progress using Trade Directories, useful though they are to historians, points to a pitfall impossible to negotiate without archive material such as Beatsons can provide. Trade Directories were produced some time after the entry had been submitted and the entry itself would merely contain what the subscriber wished it to say – some nineteenth century entries will be shown to be inaccurate, perhaps because the subscriber wished to boost his firm's image. Successive entries can also disguise the history of a works through restructuring and the forming of new partnerships, for example, in the case of the Masbrough works:

1783	W. Beatson & Co.
1817	Beatson & Close
1822	William Beatson & Co.
1828	Close & Clark
1856	William Clement Beatson
1859	W.C. Beatson
1862	William C. Beatson
1862	John G. Clark
1865	Beatson & Co.
1925	Beatson Clark & Co.

The 1828 entry is the same works with a new partnership through the marriage of William Beatson into the family of Henry Close of the glassworks at Rothwell Hague but could only be known from the family archive. In addition, Directories often omit a firm known to have existed at the time and the introduction of a previously unstated name might suggest an additional works when it is merely renaming an old one.

In 1775 at Attercliffe, Benjamin Richardson, a glassmaker, apprenticed his son to a scissormaker (Leader 1905:326). He would have worked at the glassworks advertised in the 'Sheffield Register' on 1st November, 1793, which was:

'To Be Let – A glasshouse for making Glass Bottles etc ... at Attercliffe .. near a large colliery and the turnpike road, at present in the occupation of J.Dixon'.

An 1819 survey of the area by Fairbank[2] shows 'Sarah Slater's Plot', containing '8 houses, Glass House, Stable & Gardens' (Figure 13). The circular plan and radial airways indicated on the survey suggest this was a cone furnace. The surveyor's notes state it was then in the occupation of 'Carr' but nothing further is yet known of the works and the site is now totally obscured by the later steelworks of Sanderson Kayser Ltd. However, Dixon is a familiar name amongst glassmakers and the Carr family, long established at Attercliffe, were to be involved in various Sheffield glassworks during the 1850s.

The local glass industry was now firmly established on the new national industrial pattern with its division between the owners of the assets who decided what should be produced and the operatives, skilled or otherwise, who worked as landless labourers to produce the goods. Inevitably this led to specialisation and the earlier generations of small independent producers such as at Bolsterstone and Silkstone producing small quantities of a wide variety of wares faded from the scene, no longer able to compete.

GLASS TAX

A further factor in the demise of these early works was undoubtedly the extent of State interference in the middle of the eighteenth century. The national industry had expanded to the point where, for the first time, it was not only able to supply all the home market but was moving into ever-widening areas of the global market. Such a rich and growing industry, perhaps inevitably, attracted the attentions of the Treasury again as a ready source of revenue. The granting of monopolies in exchange for payment to the King's exchequer had died with the Stuarts but in 1745 Parliament approved an Act under George II imposing a tax on glass which, with slight amendments, remained in force until withdrawn in 1845 by Queen Victoria. The Act, like the monopolies, was bitterly opposed by the glassmakers throughout its existence, not primarily for the rates of tax, severe though they were, but for the manner in which the tax was applied.

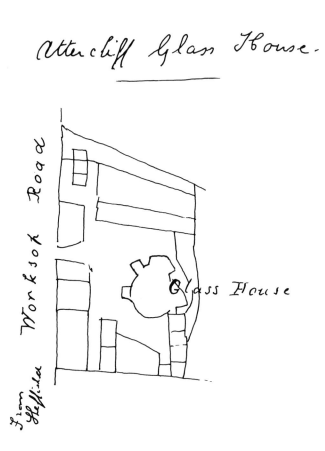

Figure 13   Attercliffe Glassworks.

It not only siphoned off profits which might otherwise have helped inspire research and innovation avoiding the stagnation in production methods which characterised the industry during the next hundred years, but controlled the actual running of every glassworks. Innovation was effectively choked.

Yet the intention of the Act had been otherwise as can be seen in the evidence taken at a Commissioners of Excise Inquiry[3] in 1835. At its core was the principle of 'drawbacks' whereby, any tax paid by the glassmaker could be clawed back (often at a profit) if the goods were exported to any colony or country, including the Channel Islands. This meant, for example, that for every hundredweight of 'common bottles' he paid 7s 0d tax but, if exported, could claim 7s 0d back.

However, if he made window glass the tax was £3 13s 6d on each hundredweight which again he could claim back if exported, unless the exported panes were

> 'regular rectangular figures not being of less dimensions than six inches in length by four inches in breadth, nor containing any part of the bullion or thick centre part'.

In this case he could claim back £4 18s 0d per hundredweight for his exports.

The different types of glass (window, plate, bottle, flint etc.) were charged at different rates and this led to a major difficulty in that

> '..manufacturers of glass are prohibited making any sort of glass.. other than flint glass, in any glass-house entered for making flint glass..'

and so for each type of glass. This was in spite of the fact that works such as Bolsterstone were clearly capable of making any type of glass in the same furnace. This was prohibited by the Act, each glassworks had to be registered for one particular type of glass.

The glassworks owner had to give twelve hours notice to the Excise Officer before charging a crucible and state the time he was to begin. The Officer had to weigh it and

> 'the turn of the scale was to be given in favour of the Crown'.

When the glass was ready:

'.. having begun to work any common bottle-metal out of any pot, must work such metal out of all the pots then charged, within sixteen hours after he shall have so begun'.

Any glass left in any crucible was thrown out as waste even though it had been taxed.

Many glassworks owners complained to the commission that, although crown glass waste, particularly the centre bulge, was too impure for re-use in crown glass, it was excellent for adding to bottle-glass cullet. The Exchequer had banned this and insisted crown glass waste be thrown away because otherwise it would make

'goods so fine it would bring them into competition with flint glass.'

The interference went even further. The Act set out the actual sizes of the lehrs and how they were to be made with

'.. sides and ends perpendicular to each other, and the bottom thereof level, and with only one mouth or entrance..'

This was intended to make the Excise Officer's task easier as he had to supervise the placing of all finished articles into the lehr for annealing so that they could be checked and counted (having been given six hours notice), lock it up and keep the key so that only he could open it. He then had to be given notice, in writing, when the articles were ready to be removed from the lehr and at what hour between six in the morning and six in the afternoon, and no other time.

Successive amendments even detailed the extensive records the owner must maintain to

'.. mark and number every workhouse, pot-chamber, pot-hole, lear, warehouse-room..'

and give the Excise Officer completely free access to every part of the glassworks at all times. Perhaps enough has been said to show the conditions which the late eighteenth century glassworks owner had to endure in operating his works yet one part of the Act was resented more than any of these regulations, namely the problem of rejects and breakages.

The tax was levied on new glass in the crucible and on the finished articles from the lehr. Unfortunately, some glass was inevitably wasted in the crucible because of the working-out time limit; the annealing process went wrong from time to time when, for example, bottles would partially melt at the neck or plate glass warp uselessly; transport of the glass to the purchaser was always hazardous given the state of roads and the problems of adequate packing in transit. But the tax paid on any faulty, damaged or broken article could not be reclaimed as it had been calculated on the weight of articles in the lehr, not numbers, even though the glassmakers worked their sales and profits by the numbers of articles. Glassworks owners at the time asserted justifiably that a 10% loss was common and complained that the method of tax collection not only greatly restricted their working methods but robbed their profits by penalising them for something over which they had only marginal control. Even modern technology and transport cannot guarantee that every piece will be annealed perfectly and arrive at its destination undamaged.

One effect of the Act which contempories could hardly have foreseen originated in the separation of 'flint' works and 'bottle' works. This lay the foundations for an aristocracy amongst glassmen which flourished in the nineteenth century and will be seen to be at the root of many of that century's disturbances and labour problems. In addition it marked a rise toward protectionism by owners and workers respectively and their dichotomy was complete.

TECHNOLOGY

The Bolsterstone furnace had held four crucibles and was no doubt efficient and economic to run. However, it was probably at the maximum size for such an operation and incapable of enlargement without loss of efficiency. Inability to increase the number of pots seriously limited its capacity to compete by volume of products in addition to the strict limits on the types and colours of glass which could be in use at any one time. Diderot (1765:105–107) acknowledged that the completely new design of the 'cone' furnace was a particularly British invention, even providing precise details on how it should be built, but its inventor is unknown. It could be argued that the 'barn' type glassworks such as Bolsterstone would require some form of chimney for the escape of fumes from the building itself but the cone is an entirely different concept. Many writers have misunderstood its function and it is not to be regarded simply as a large chimney but as an integral part of the furnace structure with the men, in effect, working within the furnace.

The large openings around the base (Figure 14) were provided with doors which, if closed, would ensure that all air entering the structure was forced through the coal bed and out through the gathering holes of the dome into the cone proper. This strong convection current created the force of the draught.

Extraction of air from the top of the cone would be aided by any wind blowing across the top, causing a lower pressure in the upper air level and helping to ensure a fairly smoke-free working atmosphere around the furnace.

In this condition, with all doors closed, the pressure of air through the coal bed created a continuous blast to create a high temperature. If left in this state it would overheat and result in total meltdown of the crucibles and sieges, a consequence not unknown. However, if any base door was open, air could enter the cone without passing through the furnace and the management of how many doors were open, and whether to windward or leeward, could regulate the furnace temperature to give a higher degree of control than had previously been possible. Its success can be measured by the fact that such 'direct' furnaces remained in use in glassmaking until the present century, were copied abroad, and not seriously challenged for a hundred and fifty years.

Unlike the tunnel lehr of the Midlands cones, local examples such as Catcliffe and Gawber appear to have a heated area sectioned off within the cone (Figure 15) suggesting a development of the earlier type of lehr at Bolsterstone (Ashurst 1970:105). Excavation at Gawber also revealed the steps into the airway used by the teaser to gain access beneath the furnace. The 5cm thick iron bars of the coal grid had been set in slots along the siege edge.

It has not been possible to calculate the intitial cost of building a cone glassworks but a double-skinned cone as at Catcliffe with its underground structure would require about 120,000 bricks. Thorpe is known to have been paying 30s a thousand bricks at Gawber in 1811 suggesting £200 or more for the cone alone. Add to this the labour costs of excavation and building; the initial stock of raw materials;

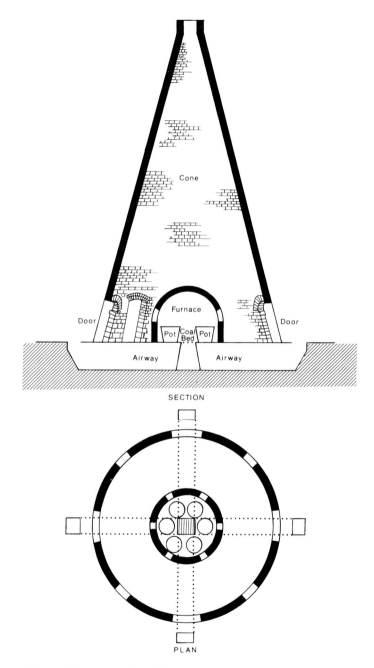

Figure 14   18th century Cone Glassworks.

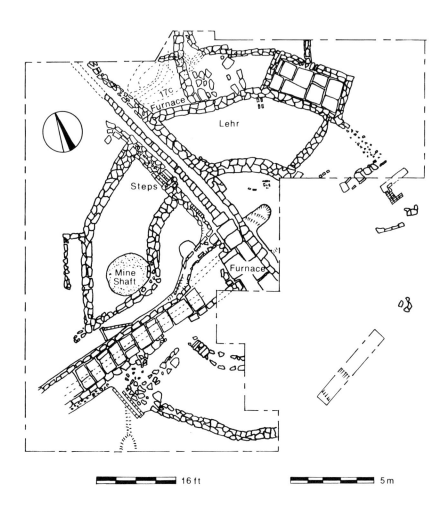

Figure 15   Gawber Glassworks – Excavation plan.

58

crucibles to be bought or specialist potters employed; transport facilities arranged and guaranteeing a constant flow of fuel – it can be seen this was no enterprise for the ordinary glassmaker, no matter how skilled, as Fenney discovered.

The absence of account books makes statistics for fuel consumption difficult but Godfrey (1975:194) calculates that production of one ton of glass consumed about six tons of coal in the late 17th century furnace. Perhaps more relevant to the cone furnace are estimates made by Diderot (1765:111) when comparing the square-built French furnace to the English cone type. He illustrates a four-pot furnace and suggests the English furnace uses one fifth less fuel than the French equivalent. As the latter consumed 90cwt per day then the English glassmaker would need to ensure a constant supply of at least 20–25 tons per week.

Most cone furnaces, however, held eight or more pots. An eight-pot cone would consume 48–50 tons per week during the three journeys of sixteen hours each and, as it was common for a works to have at least two cones, an annual supply in excess of 5000 tons of coal delivered to the works was essential. At least one furnace built in Barnsley early in the nineteenth century contained twelve crucibles emphasising the need for a constant source of good quality coal throughout the year as the furnace could never be allowed to go out.

PRODUCTS AND MARKETS

The local industry was still capable of producing a wide variety of glassware ranging from table glasses to medical ware, small phials, carboys and window glass. There were occasional specialist requests as at Gawber[4] in 1738 when Thorpe was asked

> '... whether he can blow tubes for Pendant Barometers, which are blown not truly cylindrical but with a base something broader, – though very little, – than the top, – or in other words something conical.'

However, the main output of the local eighteenth century works was undoubtedly bottles for beverages, mainly wine and mineral waters. Their reputation was such that the 1790 Universal British Directory states –

'A glass manufactory of black bottles is also carried on near this town [Barnsley] superior to any of the kind elsewhere.'

The origins of this dark 'English' bottle are in doubt but must have become fairly common in the 1630s and by the Restoration in 1660 had virtually supplanted the stone bottle which, until then, had been the sole means of storing liquids. The speed with which glass replaced stone bottles was partly due to fashion and its pleasant appearance but no doubt helped by what appears to be the only part of the tax legislation approved by the glassmakers which put a higher discriminatory tax on stone bottles to give glass bottles a clearer field to attack the market.

Throughout the later seventeenth and the eighteenth centuries the bottle underwent a series of design changes following a sequence proposed by Noel-Hume (1961) from excavations in Virginia (USA) augmented by more recent work at Oxford (Haslam 1984). Local examples illustrate the general changes in design (Figure 16).

The general evolution from squat globular to tall cylindrical is not disputed though a detailed and accurately dated sequence is unlikely to be possible because of regional variations to which precise dates cannot be ascribed in the absence of documentary evidence. Examples from local excavations and collections on display in the South Yorkshire museums illustrate the general development during which one major change should be noted.

In its early days the glass bottle merely replaced the function of the stone bottle whereby it would be taken to the cellar to be filled with wine or beer from a barrel then brought to the table. However, in the later part of the eighteenth century the technique was adopted of storing wines etc. actually in the bottle which had then to lie on its side, to keep the stopper moist and expanded, ensuring it remained airtight. This was not possible with the globular shape and the trend quickly emerged in the last quarter of the century to make bottles taller and cylindrical – the modern shape in fact which has remained unchanged.

The stopper was originally wood, later cork, and was tied to the neck with wire hooked around the string rim. A later, nineteenth century, modification gave the interior of the neck a waist so that the cork expanded after insertion and did away with the need for wiring,

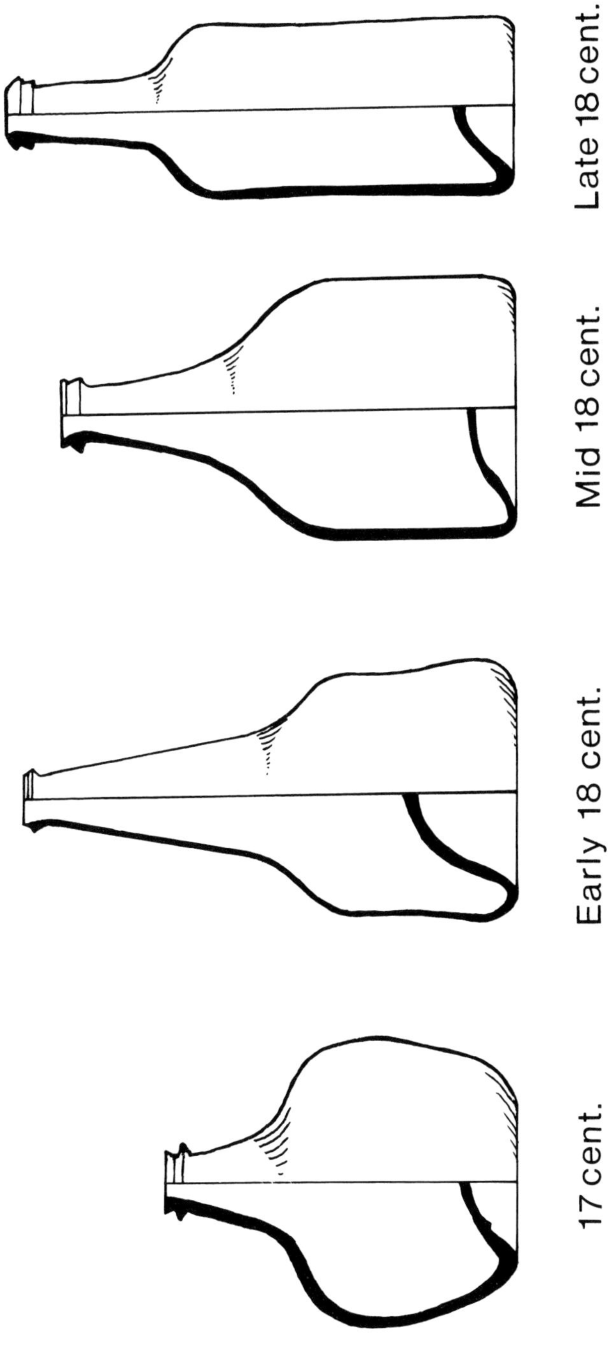

Figure 16   Evolution of wine bottles

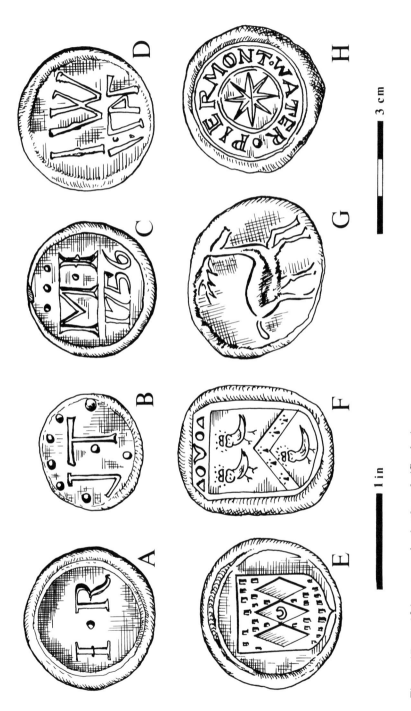

Figure 17 18th century wine bottle seals (Gawber)

making the string rim redundant. It is retained merely as a decorative feature except for the more effervescent champagne wines.

Shortly after the introduction of glass bottles the glassmakers realised that here was a new untapped market in the form of personalised bottles which carried a seal requested by the purchaser. The seal was made by pressing a small baked clay mould, on which the design had been carved (in reverse), into a small blob of glass applied to the shoulder or body of the bottle as it was being finished off and still soft.

Examples from the eighteenth century Gawber works show some of the various forms this seal could take (Figure 17):

A & B	plain initials;
C & D	initials with a date;
E & F	coat of arms for the gentry;
G	animal perhaps representing an inn sign;
H	specialist bottles for spa water designed specifically for the Bad Piermont spa water imported from Germany.

In making the stamp for seal 'D' the carver clearly forgot to create a negative and the design came out in reverse.

It should be noted, however, that any date on such a seal must be treated cautiously as it probably bears no relation to the date of manufacture of the bottle. It is more likely to be an anniversary of some kind or even the vintage of the contents (Ruggles-Brise 1949). A Gawber bottle bearing the seal 'IF 1745' preserved in the Sheffield City Museum is a case in point. It would have been made for John Fothergill of Pickering in North Yorkshire but the shape of bottle places it very late in the eighteenth century and not the 1745 of the seal.

Late in the century it became common practice to blow the bottles in a mould which could incorporate the name of the firm as advertisement. This should also be treated with caution as many firms produced bottles for others who were solely involved as bottlers of mineral water etc. and it is their name on the bottle, not the maker. To overcome this the bottle manufacturers began to include their name or logo on the base of the bottle and, as the design often changed over the years, can offer a means of dating the bottle if these changes of

Beatson Clark	
Stairfoot, Barnsley	
Rotherham, South Yorkshire	
Canning Town Glass	
Swinton, Yorkshire	C.T.G.
Queensborough, Kent	C.T.G.
Redfearn National Glass Ltd.	
Monk Bretton Works Barnsley, South Yorkshire	
Redfearn National Glass Ltd.	
Fishergate, York	
Glastics Ltd. **Trent Valley Glassworks**	
Hatton, Derbyshire	
Waterstone Glassware **Wath-upon-Dearne** Nr. Rotherham	

Figure 18   Specimen modern logos.

Rockware Glass Limited

Heatland Glass Works
Knottingly, West Yorkshire

Portland Factory
Irvine, Ayshire

St Helens, Merseyside

Wheatley, Doncaster

United Glass Containers Ltd.

Alloa, Scotland — U8

Castleford, Yorkshire — U4

Harlow, Essex — U0

Kinghorn, Scotland — U7

New Cross, London — U1

Peasley, St. Helens
Merseyside — U9

date are known. Examples of recent South Yorkshire logos are shown in Figure 18.

The industry was unlikely to have gained the national reputation for its excellent bottles noted earlier unless it had served a national market. The John Fothergill bottle does give a slight indication of the distribution range for the local glassmakers and excavations in central London have discovered evidence from seals that Gawber bottles were on the London market.

This works also seems to have become established internationally. Documentary proof of this is now impossible to obtain as no eighteenth century records of the works survive and the relevant Excise documents were destroyed in the London blitz of the last war. However, excavations in Virginia produced a considerable volume of glassware, particularly bottles, on which Noel-Hume based the development series. Comparison with the Gawber samples, particularly octagonal bottles, suggested a possible link and analysis of the glass was sufficient to give a strong indication that the bottles exported to the colony had originated in South Yorkshire, probably being shipped through Liverpool or Bristol. Unfortunately the Port Books give only quantities, not place of origin of the exports, so proof is still elusive.

The Gawber works was, however, landlocked and although within a hundred yards of the Wakefield–Sheffield Turnpike any transport of bulk glass products over any great distance would be hazardous. The disincentive of the glass tax, with no relief for breakages, would be a strong influence when the Thorpe family decided in 1824 to abandon glassmaking to concentrate on coal mining.

Catcliffe was making flint and crown glass but the nature of the products is unknown. Attercliffe was a bottle works.

The Beatson works at Masbrough diversified from bottle production with its two cones designated as 'Crown' (window glass) and 'Flint' glass. The firm's archives show an extensive range of products in 1817 most of which must equally represent the eighteenth century range though they cause some problems now as to their purpose:

Antiguglars	Bird Boxes	Corals & Daffys
Lumps	Fish Globes	Goblets
Muffineers	Patti pans	Syllabubs
French Lamp Globes	Lacemakers Lights	

66

Figure 19   18th century Masbrough Glassworks, Rotherham

The canal at Masbrough played a major role in the continuing prosperity of the works, offering a safe mode of transport for glass and raw materials so that it was firmly established to compete successfully during the dramatic expansion of the region's glass industry in the next century.

Alan Clark, Chairman of the Company in the 1950s stressed its importance (1980:21)

> 'Coal and sand all came in by canal via a bridge or gantry over the intervening railway. We occupied the site before the railway ever came, so were able to insist that there should be continued access to the canal. It was a regular weekly task to unload the barges of some 60 tons capacity, the largest size which could travel along the canal from Goole with sand, [from Kings Lynn] and from the local coalfields with fuel.'

CHAPTER 5

19TH CENTURY EXPANSION

HISTORY

British industry underwent great changes during the nineteenth century – changes which together have been summarised as an Industrial Revolution. Whether it is a suitable description and what were the elements which came together to create this change, or even when it could be said the so-called 'revolution' began, are still the topic of much debate by historians.

The population of about nine millions at the 1801 census doubled by 1851 and doubled again by 1901. During this time the shift of population from countryside to town was most marked. Where only one fifth lived in towns at 1801, the 1851 census showed for the first time more people living in towns than the countryside and by 1911 the towns contained four fifths of the population.

A major magnet for this drift was the reorganisation of manufacture which saw the decline of the cottage industries and the growth of factory production. Many forces, political, economic and social, powered the engine of these changes and, whether summarised as the spirit of the age or drive for markets, they all conspired to encourage invention, innovation and expansion with a growing source of labour to draw on.

Perhaps the two greatest changes emerging during this industrial reorganisation were the unprecedented improvements in communications with the canal /river system completed by the early decades of the century augmented by a growing railway network and secondly the increasing role of machines in production. Without these two there would have been no 'industrial revolution' to debate and the effects of both are nowhere better illustrated than in the nineteenth century glass industry.

The middle of the century saw perhaps the most important catalyst to affect glass production since the banning of wood when, in 1845, the Tax on Glass was repealed with its consequence of free trade and expansion that the glassworks owners had long sought. The effects were dramatic nationally and are mirrored in the changes in South Yorkshire as the graph illustrates, particularly in the second half of the century (Figure 20).

During the first half of the century South Yorkshire, in common with the national industry, had seen little change. The Gawber works closed in 1824, Attercliffe and Catcliffe struggled on, the latter with its fresh injection of capital when taken over by Blunn & Booth, producing bottles as well as phials and coloured glass. The Masbrough works quietly expanded to concentrate on medical and chemical glassware.

One new works was founded in the region, at Worsbrough, to the east of Barnsley on the banks of the Dearne & Dove canal. It later became known simply as Wood Brothers. Little is known of its original founders – Usherwood, Barron, Cartwright and Perkes – but Perkes was recorded as a 'Glass Manufacturer' from Worcester in the 1851 Worsbrough census return. No early, and very few later, records of the firm have survived but the foundation date of 1828 given by Barker (1925:327), repeated by other writers such as Hill (1982:32), may be in doubt as the Census shows Richard Perkes had a daughter born in Worcester in 1831 and a son in Worsbrough in 1833. Writing in 1872, Wilkinson (1872:222) is probably more accurate when he says the works '... have been carried on here for a period of upwards of 40 years..' giving a foundation date of 1832.

During 1834 the partnership changed with the arrival of the brothers John and James Wood, glass manufacturers from Wordsley, Staffordshire, who took over the firm with Perkes. John Wood was the commercial manager, James the glass cutter and Perkes the glass maker. Other members of the Wood family were also working in the Dudley area until the 1840s (Buckley 1927). Another brother, William, had left Stourbridge in the 1840s for the Baccarat works in France but his son Eugene returned to England in 1851 to join the Worsbrough works and introduced etching, gilding and the deep cutting of heavy lead glass. His father returned in 1854 and another son, Alphonse, in 1870. It was truly the Wood Brothers' glassworks.

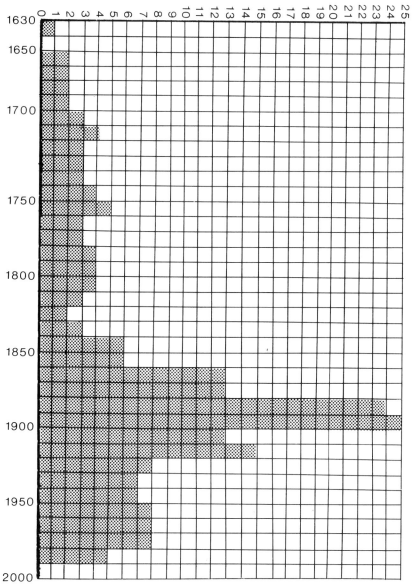

Figure 20   South Yorkshire Glassworks – Frequency graph.

The firm prospered as a flint glassworks with all the advantages of skilled technical managers and an ideal site which had, in addition to the canal basin alongside, a line of the new railway passing through the works at the Worsbrough Goods Yard (Joy 1975:190) and a short road leading to the Wakefield–Sheffield turnpike. New coal mines had been sunk to the south and east. Across the railway line were the lime kilns of the Jessop brothers, the largest in the area, who obtained their limestone from quarries at Consibrough and Knottingley, the latter being better quality costing 8% more.

In 1871 the ground lease expired and, for reasons yet unknown, the landlord, W.B.Martin of Worsbrough Hall, refused to renew it. The firm built a new works in 1872 at Hoyle Mill, on the north-eastern outskirts of Barnsley alongside the Barnsley Canal and with its own railway sidings. It prospered as a family business until the mid-20th century, even establishing a branch at Wombwell but, in 1981, following trading difficulties, the Wood family decided to sell. As no purchaser came forward the works was closed and the site cleared leaving no surviving trace.

The final fate of the original works sited at Worsbrough is less clear. It had specialised in flint glass which was cut and ground on site and, according to Barker (1925:329), glassmaking ceased in 1873 though products were brought back from the new Hoyle Mill works for grinding at Worsbrough until 1874. It is known, however, that Jessop Lime Kilns continued to deliver normal quantities of lime to the Worsbrough site until 1875 in addition to supplying the new works from 1873. Perhaps some of the workers tried to continue glass production independently, particularly as the 1881 Census shows glassworkers still living in Worsbrough.

After the foundation of the Wood Brothers' works there was a pause in the further development of the local glass industry until the repeal of the glass tax in mid-century which not only initiated expansion in the already established areas around Barnsley and Sheffield but eastward towards Mexborough and associated villages along the South Yorkshire Navigation canal (see Figure 1). The new works were created by skilled men setting up on their own or by repeated subdivision of newly-formed partnerships. Frequent changes of trading name together with changes of ownership and partnership present an often confusing kaleidoscope across the region, the shifting patterns of which will probably never be completely understood.

Some prospered, many soon fell by the wayside. Unfortunately for the historian the great majority of these nineteenth century works were of such brief existence as to be almost ephemeral. They have disappeared leaving no trace on the ground and virtually no archival record to fill in the story which, at present, offers the merest glimpse. No doubt they were set up in the full confidence of a growth industry in an expanding market. However, events were rapidly to overtake them as the industry underwent a violent change from the world of the glass craftsman, in which their confidence lay, to an alien machine world which made large-scale capital demands in the move to industrial mechanisation by the end of the century.

The existence of many of these works can only be known at present from sources such as Trade Directories and, unless further evidence comes to light, such entries with their inherent unreliability must remain the only guide to their existence. The Gazetteer lists all the currently identified glassworks but the biographical notes in the remainder of this chapter represent a selection of those works which made a significant contribution to the advance of the South Yorkshire industry and for which firm evidence has survived.

The new developments in the Mexborough area provide an ideal example of the partnership fragmentation which commonly occurred resulting in the confusion of repeated changes of trading name and taking the same name of a works to another area.

In 1842 Ben Micklethwaite mortgaged his Mexborough Flint Glass Works, a seven pot furnace by the Don Navigation Canal, and was followed by George Bache who went bankrupt in 1849. Joseph Barron, then manager at Worsbrough after working at Hunslet and Whitwood, took over the works with his sons and Ben Rylands, John and James Tillotson and Joseph Wilkinson. In 1850 it had been renamed the Don Works.

A New Don Works was built in 1857 by Joseph Barron's son, also Joseph, who went bankrupt in 1867 when he sold out to James Montague. He in turn was soon taken over by Hartley Barron, William Roebuck and Joseph and Charles Bullock.

Hartley Barron built a further Don Works at nearby Denaby which was abandoned when it sank below the river level through mining subsidence.

About 1876 Joseph Barron's son, Thomas, returned to the 'old' Don Works and renamed it Phoenix, a name under which the Barron family traded until selling out in 1989.

In 1852 the earlier partnership at Mexborough Flint Glass Works had divided and Rylands, Tillotson and Wilkinson left the 'old' Don Works to set up the Swinton glassworks which later became known as the South Yorkshire Glass Company. This, in turn, became Dale Brown in 1933 and by 1962 was known as Canning Town Glass, part of United Glass Containers under which latter name it traded in the 1980s. From the Barron family papers it appears that the Dale Brown company started another works in 1913 taking over a glassworks which had been derelict for three years. Unfortunately they fail to state the location of this works.

The confusion of glassworks names is further illustrated in the Attercliffe, Sheffield, developments. The original eighteenth century works on 'Sarah Slater's Plot' had ceased by mid-nineteenth century and Melling Carr & Co. began producing 'flint and green glass' at a new works nearby in Faraday Road beside the river Don. They called it the Don Glass Works. However, it was taken over in 1861 by Thomas Edward Mycock making flint glass and by 1872 was occupied by William Langwell. The latter moved to Cleveland Square in Darnall Road where the works was referred to as Langwell Brothers but still trading under the Don Works label.

The 1891 OS 1/500 map shows this to have been an extensive works overlying the earlier glassworks on the Sarah Slater Plot but by 1920 the site had been cleared when the new Sanderson Kayser steelworks was built, totally obscuring the glassworks sites. The Langwell brothers had set up additional works in Joiner Street and Stanley Street trading variously as Langwell Brothers and Langwell & Co., being last mentioned in the White Trade Directory of 1905.

Another new works in Sheffield which was to be significant in the next century was that founded by P.T.Turner in Sussex Street in 1890.

One of the partners in the Swinton glassworks noted above was Ben Rylands who left there in 1867 to build his own works at Stairfoot, near Barnsley, which he called the Hope Glass Works (Figure 21). He was succeeded in 1881 by his son, Dan, whose contribution to the British glass industry in general is perhaps underestimated. He had a genius for innovation and improvement but it must be agreed with Turner (1938:252) that 'his inventiveness did

Figure 21   Hope Glass Works – Barnsley

not meet with its just recognition and reward.' During the late 1880s Rylands held ninety four patents relating to furnace design and glass-making machinery. Possibly his greatest contribution which gained international recognition for the British industry was the development with Hiram Codd of the glass-marble stoppered mineral water bottle to be discussed later.

The site Rylands chose for his works was ideal, with ample space for expansion, railways passing through it and the Barnsley canal alongside. It became sufficiently profitable for Rylands to lease a second works in 1872, the Dearne & Dove Glassworks, at Wombwell.

Production problems to be discussed later led to the works closing in 1927. The site was cleared before being purchased by Beatson Clark in 1929 who built a new glassworks additional to their Masbrough works and remains currently in production.

Another major works established in the later nineteenth century grew up on the Barnsley canal near the site of the town's old corn mill. James Wragg built the original works in 1861 but, having little success, he gave it up to become a pork butcher in 1862 and the glassworks was bought by the brothers Joshua and Samuel Redfearn, trading as 'Redfearn Brothers' at the Old Mill Glassworks. They enlarged the works and concentrated entirely on containers – bottles and jars – but continuously adapted the production methods to the changing technology with such success that, in 1895, they were able to take over an additional works at Aldham Bridge, Wombwell, operated by Dickinson since 1872.

Thirty glassworks have been positively identified as operating at various times towards the close of the nineteenth century in South Yorkshire. Some were new and others were extensions of works already established in the West Yorkshire area such as Kilner Brothers arriving in Conisbrough in 1844 to set up the Providence Glass Works making the famous Kilner Preserve jar; but the list cannot be closed as being complete. Additional works may be hiding under the confusion of names as, for example, at Aldham Bridge noted above. From the Redfearn papers it is known as 'Aldham Bridge' when absorbed in 1872 but the Jessop Lime Kilns were still supplying the 'Dickinson & Hammerton Aldham Glass Works' in 1875. It cannot be said with certainty if they are the same works or two separate firms with Dickinson as sole owner of one and part owner of the other. Many such problems remain but so few archives have survived that a full answer may never be known.

The location of the majority of these works and many of their names have long been forgotten. It remains possible, however, that glassworks sprang up which were so ephemeral that they even lacked a name by which to be forgotten.

The first edition OS map (1850) shows a small circle at SE/353044 in Worsbrough, about two miles north of the Wood Brothers' glassworks. Elderly residents recall the demolition of a brick cone early this century to clear the site for estate houses, the waste building material being used to fill a swampy area under the houses. The site now offers no evidence other than a few burnt stones. Across the road from the marked circle is a spring known as 'Bottle Spring' and the 1881 Census shows glassworkers still living at this edge of the parish at least six years after the Wood Brothers' works had closed. Between 1866–1867 the Jessop Lime Kilns were supplying large quantities of lime to the then owner of the site, Rev.W.Elmhirst, but the Elmhirst family papers provide no further enlightenment.

On such delicate evidence may a glassworks of the late nineteenth century expansion have slipped from memory unnoticed.

TECHNOLOGY

Cone furnaces continued in use throughout the century though comparison of the early Rotherham Glassworks (Figure 19) and a later nineteenth century etching (Figure 22) show a development had been a widening of the base to provide an increased working area. The cones held twelve closed pots, each containing one ton of glass. After charging with a new 'batch' they were left twenty four hours to melt and, as a measure of the still-prevailing attitude of craft magic in the industry, their founder's cure for bubbly glass was to 'stick in a banana skin or a quart of water'. One of these Beatson Clark cones continued in production to the 1920s.

Wood Brothers had two small eight pot cone furnaces at Worsbrough and, on their new site at Hoyle Mill they had '.. an eight pot furnace with 60 foot conical chimney of the Stourbridge type built by Ingrams of Birmingham' (Hill 1982). In 1874 another furnace was added which was based on the Boetius design developed in Hanover

Figure 22   Rotherham Glassworks – Beatson Clark

incorporating the regenerative principle seen earlier at Bolsterstone. This used some of the furnace atmosphere to pre-heat the incoming air and increase efficiency. Unfortunately it was too efficient and ran out of control – 'The siege of the furnace was completely destroyed, the pots melted...and the whole thing made into a lump of rubbish all in the space of one week – before we had scarcely had time to get any work out of the furnace' (Hodkin 1953:32).

Their troubles continued, but were not unique to the Wood's management and must be seen as representing the problems being faced by all glassmakers during this major step forward into a new, mass production, technology. They rebuilt a traditional direct fired furnace but included an automatic Frisbie coal feed, hoping this would give better control over the furnace temperature which had always been the problem with a hand-fed cone furnace. It failed. In its place was built what was, by now, an old-fashioned furnace which could assure a longer life, need minimum running repairs but was adequate. It remained in use to the 1930s.

They tried another regenerative furnace burning gas as fuel in 1890 to increase capacity. It was lit on 15th November and exploded, blowing out the ends. The idea was abandoned and the furnace converted to an eighteen (later twenty four) pot standard furnace.

Despite these stirrings of the imminent introduction of a new shape to the industry it should be noted that the actual methods of working within the glassworks had changed little over the centuries. It was still based on the 'chair' and the production of bottles typify the organisation as shown in the interior sketch of the Aston Glassworks, used here in the absence of any local illustration (Figure 23).

The team (or 'chair') making bottles consisted usually of five workers with the 'gaffer' sitting in his chair as in the centre of the drawing. He was in charge of the team and carried out the final stages of processing. A 'gatherer' can be seen at a furnace hole taking a gather of glass on his blowing iron. The 'gob' of glass would then be rolled on a marver – a smooth slab of iron or stone (not illustrated) – to homogenise the glass and remove air bubbles before passing to the 'blower' who would create the bottle body shape. This might be free blown as shown to the right, or blown into a mould if, say, an octagonal bottle was required. Another worker attached an iron bar, the 'pontil' onto the base of the bottle and, by applying a drop of water

Figure 23a   18th century glassworks (Aston) – interior

Figure 23b   18th century glassworks (Aston) – exterior

using a soaked strip of wood, the 'wetter off' snapped off the blowing iron.

Now attached to the pontil, the bottle was transferred to the gaffer who, using the flat arms of his 'chair', kept the bottle turning as he worked, otherwise, in its soft state, it might collapse. He would trim its shape, finish the neck and add the string rim and any seal that was required. An iron rod was inserted in the bottle mouth by an assistant boy and the gaffer could snap off the pontil by applying a flash of water (leaving the so-called 'pontil mark' on the base).

The finished bottle was then taken to the lehr for annealing in the manner shown by the small boy in the right foreground. Boys in the team had to remove the waste glass ('moils') from the end of blowing irons and pontils by dipping them in a water tank as shown on the floor to the left. The working ends of the irons were then placed in the furnace as at the left side gathering hole to heat up ready for the next gather. Such a team would be expected to produce about 150 finished bottles an hour.

This method of working in the glass industry was so firmly established that any hope of increasing production depended on two factors; glass had to be available constantly to avoid the delays caused when waiting for a fresh batch to be ready and, secondly, a way had to be found to remove the grip the gaffers and blowers had on the system by becoming less dependent on their skill.

A depression in the industry towards the end of the century and labour problems resulting in the 1893 lock-out made it not the most auspicious time for such changes but the first problem had been solved in the 1850s in Germany by Siemens' invention of the 'tank furnace'. (Figure 24)

It is first recorded in the West Yorkshire area at the Kilner works in Castleford in 1873 but rapidly spread throughout the South Yorkshire region, though not without its problems. Most disasters have gone unrecorded but again, by a chance documentary survival, Wood Brothers can be instanced when, as late as 1929, they changed their number one furnace to a 'small recuperative tank .. the temperature was raised in an attempt to free the glass from seed [bubbles]. After three or four weeks the whole structure melted down and collapsed.' (Hill 1982).

However, as the technology was mastered, the tank became universal for the bulk of glass manufacture which required repetitive

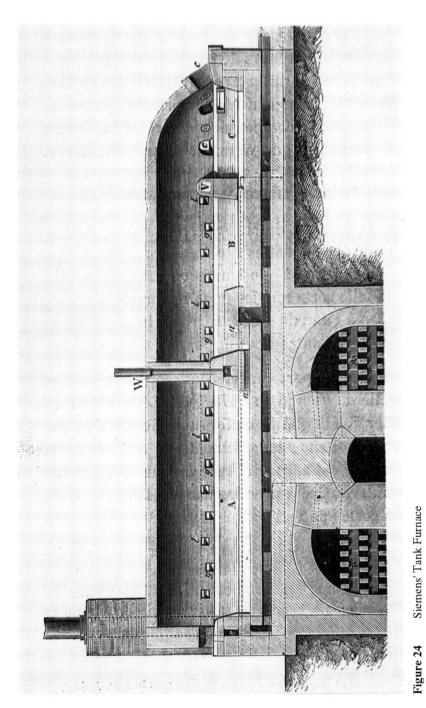

Figure 24   Siemens' Tank Furnace

production and its success was paradoxically a major factor in the later decline of the industry so far as the number of glassworks is concerned, even though the quantities produced rose dramatically. For the glassworker it was to cause the greatest change in his working and social life he was ever to confront as will be seen in Chapter 7.

Glass had been melted in crucibles since its beginnings. Even though it has been seen that nineteenth century crucibles could each hold a ton of glass it still meant that when the team of five had exhausted it during the average sixteen hour working period they had to stop work until it was replenished. The crucible would be recharged with fresh raw materials but then had to be left 24–36 hours to melt during which the team did no work.

In the Siemens tank furnace illustration (Figure 24) (Peligot 1877:416) the raw materials fed into one end (left on the diagram) steadily flowed to the other end to be gathered continuously (Gunther 1958:1). Glass was gathered through a series of holes in the semi-circular domed end (the holes shown along the sides were vent holes for gases). This led to a number of complaints by the glassmen that, with the same number of workers as with the circular furnace, they now had no room to work with only half a circle. The situation was exacerbated by the workforce often being increased to take advantage of the greater quantity of glass available and, whereas 30 was common before, up to 180 was not uncommon at the tank end.

The immediate advantage of the tank was that with glass continuously available work need never stop once night shifts were introduced though, at first, the tank was worked out each day. In addition its size was only limited by the heating capacity to keep it at the required temperature. Twenty four hour production was not only possible, but desirable.

Attempts to automate the production of bottles using the crucible system were balked by the need to collect glass manually at the gathering hole then convey it to a machine. The tank created the incentive to develop a means of transferring molten glass automatically to machines to eliminate manual work.

In 1885 Dan Rylands invented such an apparatus to feed molten glass to a semi-automatic bottle-making machine. His intention was to dispense with the employment of a skilled gatherer but it was 'only partially successful; it was probably a little before its time' but was perfected in 1901 by Homer Brooke (Singer 1958:676).

However, the necessity to keep the tank at the optimum temperature created its own problem with regard to fuel. Coal was found to be unsatisfactory as even the Frisbie automatic fuel beds which took coal the length of the tank were unable to maintain a reliable steady temperature throughout. The solution was found in gas as the fuel and a prospectus of Dan Rylands Ltd for 1888 includes:

two large continuous regenerative glass melting furnaces
three smaller of the same
two ordinary coal furnaces
forty two annealing furnaces
eight Rylands patent gas producers
sixteen gas producers

It is of interest to note here that, although it took place in the 1920s, Beatson Clark also found coal to be unsatisfactory and they designed a tank to burn their own producer gas. However, gas was then being produced from coal and the new Rotherham Gas Works was investing in laying a pipe to supply gas to a chemical works in nearby Rawmarsh. This was tapped into by Beatson Clark to try using this new 'town gas' which was cheap, being considered a waste product in obtaining coke from coal mainly for local ironworks. It was an instant success and the producer gas idea was abandoned. The firm became the first to use coal gas as a fuel but was soon followed throughout the industry.

The Siemens gas-fired furnace became almost universal and has changed little albeit North Sea gas or oil replaced the old 'town gas'.

The first real breach in the hold the gaffer and chair system had on the industry, particularly with regard to bottle production, came with the invention in 1886 of the semi-automatic machine by H.M.Ashley, an iron founder of Ferrybridge. He went bankrupt developing the idea but a modified version finally came into production in Castleford in 1887 and rapidly spread into South Yorkshire. Under the chair system the team of five was expected to produce about 150 bottles per hour – the Ashley machine required just two men, both unskilled labourers, one to gather and one to operate the machine, but could produce 200 bottles an hour. The savings to the owner were obvious but, to the glassworkers disastrous and the move to automation was resented and resisted strongly as will be seen in Chapter 7.

Figure 25   Wood Brothers Glassworks – Hoyle Mill (Barnsley)

The new furnaces spelled the end of the English 'cone' glassworks as heat control became more a matter of turning taps rather than opening doors and shovelling coal. Cone technology was now redundant after a hundred and fifty years.

For the prospective glass entrepreneur, however, these new furnaces meant he need no longer be dependent on the large railway/canal system to cope with the vast quantities of coal fuel. Geographical determination for siting was eliminated and, although the industry was by now firmly seated on the eastern reaches of the rich Yorkshire coalfield, any new works need only be a gaspipe away and could be just one pot or a series of tanks – size was now largely irrelevant.

Any new glassworks buildings reflected the change in working practice by becoming rectangular 'sheds' lacking any distinction and blending into the general industrial scene as rows of workshops virtually indistinguishable from those of any other industry.

At the end of the century the Beatson Clark works had retained some of the character of an eighteenth century glass works mixed in with the new, but the Wood Brothers' Glass Works at Barnsley had become what is now the idealised picture of the Victorian 'factory' with nothing to differentiate it from any other kind of factory.

PRODUCTS AND MARKETS

'Freedom from tax, demand for drinks containers, bottling jars for fruits, pickles etc led to Yorkshire as a great seat of the bottle trade by the mid-1860s'.[1] Two of the region's works, however, aimed for a more specialist market.

At Beatson Clark, in addition to the clear glass jars for household use, their major contribution to the industry was in the field of pharmaceutical and medical glassware. The wide range of lotion, chemical and cosmetic containers in a variety of colours which developed has been continued and expanded to the present day.

Repeal of the Glass Tax encouraged glassmakers to increase the glass thickness. Wood Brothers originally took advantage of this to develop a wide range of cut-glass quality crystal ware and in 1871 they employed twelve cutters, one engraver and one carver compared to seven glassmakers. They were able to join other English

ROTHERHAM GLASS WORKS

WHITE AND COLOURED FLINT GLASS.
RECESS LABELLED GOODS.

Figure 26   19th century specimen product range – Beatson & Co..

glassworks in the challenge to imported Irish cut-glass which had never been subject to the tax. Although the style was much decried by Ruskin who thought 'all cut glass is barbarous' it dominated Victorian household glass and introduced a new artistic approach to glass decoration, displacing the traditional engraving embellishment which Wood Brothers had also produced. Examples of their products were displayed at the 1851 Crystal Palace exhibition, an epergne now preserved at Barnsley's Cawthorne Museum being awarded the gold medal.

Though the evidence is scanty, a similar cut-glass industry must have developed in Sheffield. Melling Carr is listed in a Trade Directory as makers and cutters of flint glass and Langwell Brothers had the 'Nursery Steam Grinding Wheel'. A number of other grinding wheels primarily intended for steel work are to be associated with glass grinding and cutting which suggests they were taking in work from the glassmakers under contract (Crossley 1989:38,65). It should be noted that the designation 'flint' glass appears to have undergone a slight change in meaning during the century. Originally applied to glass made from ground flint, then later used to denote lead crystal, a term 'white flint' had become common which referred to a clear (white) glass of the alkali/lime type. Its use was widespread in jars, chemical ware etc and, in the absence of other records, it is often unclear precisely what was made at some of the works listed in Trade Directories as 'flint glass houses'.

Towards the end of the century 'pressed' glass was introduced which imitated the cut-glass but could be produced cheaply by unskilled operators using a machine press.

But bottles of all shapes and sizes remained the core of the South Yorkshire industry. No figures are available to indicate output for the region but in 1862 the 47 bottle houses in Newcastle produced 4,220,000 dozen bottles annually (Turner 1938:118) suggesting at least 1,000,000 dozen annually from the 15 local bottle works.

A minor revolution in the bottle industry occurred in 1870 with the invention by Hiram Codd of a bottle to hold the aerated waters which had become popular. He developed the design in association with Richard Barrett in London (Talbot 1974:46–54) but by 1874 they were being made by Ben Rylands at the Hope Glass Works in Barnsley as the 'Codd Proper' or 'Codd No.4' and in 1877 Codd and Rylands went into partnership. After Ben died in 1881 Dan Rylands became co-partner but the association was somewhat fraught and, when the original patents had expired in 1885, Rylands brought out an improved version which led to legal disputes.

The design was based on the use of a glass marble within the neck of the bottle which, under pressure from the aerated contents, was forced up against a rubber ring in the neck. The marble could be pushed down using a wooden peg to release the contents and pinching along the bottle sides, prevented the marble falling into the bottom. The Rylands 1871 patent included a further constriction to prevent the marble re–entering the neck when pouring out (Figure 27).

Manufacture of the marble became almost a second industry and Rylands had works in London solely for the purpose but Tomlinsons at Stairfoot near Rylands' Hope Works also made it a speciality. The technical reason for special production lay in the fact that the marble had to be inserted when the bottle was still hot and soft so that the neck could then be narrowed to prevent the marble falling out. This meant the marble had to be made from glass of a higher melting point than the bottle glass to avoid sticking during insertion.

Other glass works throughout the country took advantage of the popularity of the 'Codd' bottle to bring out variants, even one in Barnsley itself, two miles from the Rylands works.

> 'Mr.T. Sutcliffe, owner of the Oaks Glass Works ... after much thought and no light display of ingenuity, has succeeded in inventing a glass stopper which will do away with the necessity for corking and wiring'.

This was 1875, only five years after Codd's patent. It appears to have gone unchallenged and was fully reported in the Barnsley Chronicle of 24 July 1875. Attention at the demonstration seems to have concentrated, not on the marble closure, but the considerable increase attainable in the rate of filling bottles with aerated water using the marble closure system. A new machine was shown which in unskilled hands could fill 70–80 dozen bottles and hour which was double the old 'string and cork' method.

During the century the 'black glass' bottle for which the region was originally famous had become more the province of the Lancashire (St.Helens) and Newcastle glassworks. It was replaced locally with the new pale green bottle which emerged dominant throughout the

Figure 27   Codd Bottle.

Fruit   Bottling

In the   Home.

KILNER BROTHERS, Ltd.
CONISBOROUGH,
ARE MANUFACTURERS OF ALL
DESCRIPTIONS of GLASS BOTTLES

Fruit Bottling in the Home.

There is a growing practice amongst housewives of preparing in summer a stock of Bottled Fruit ready for that part of the year when fresh fruit cannot be obtained, and nothing can be more useful or acceptable in the home menu.

With suitable Jars this can be done easily, and the
KILNER FRUIT JAR
fulfils this purpose exactly.

It is of **English Manufacture**, made in Pale Green Glass, and fitted with Glass Lid, Rubber Ring and Screw Band. Perfectly Air-tight. Four sizes—1, 2, 3 and 4 lb. with Wide Mouth (2-in. inside diameter) suitable for large fruit. The fittings are all the same size and are therefore interchangeable. Only Glass in contact with the contents.

"Pale Green" Glass is composed of new raw material, and is therefore sound and strong.

Altogether a most Serviceable Jar.

Figure 28   Kilner Jar.

South Yorkshire industry which, by the 1860s, was being nationally recognised as 'a great seat of the bottle trade'.

However, another new product of note in the latter part of the century was the 'Kilner Jar' produced at the works of Kilner Brothers in Conisbrough and Thornhill Lees which soon received wide acclaim and is still sought today (Figure 28).

Before the days of refrigerators the preservation of food was a constant worry to the housewife. The Victorians developed sophisticated methods of preserving jams, pickles, soft fruit etc using jars over which a waxed paper cover could be tied round the lip. The Kilner jar with its metal screw cap was not only superior to the paper cover but opened a whole new field which housewives quickly exploited as a range of foods could be cooked in the jar and the perfect seal of the cap prevented any deterioration for months. Bottle preservation techniques, to be reliably successful, required fine sugar and the great upsurge in food preservation toward the end of the century was considerably helped by the abolition of the Sugar Tax in 1875 making it cheap enough for all (Davies 1989:93).

The markets for the region's range of products was no longer restricted to its growing industrial towns but could reach out via its canal, rail and improving road network. Direct links to the east coast ports of Hull and Goole took an increasing volume of exports. Matsumura (1983:17) quotes the value of national exports of flint glass doubling from £718,000 in 1850–4 to £1,511,000 by 1870–4 and, although the surviving excise records for exports of glass give only the national figures, the area's proportion may be judged from the employment of 16.7% of the nations glassworkers in South and West Yorkshire. The destination of these exports can be seen from the answers given at a Parliamentary enquiry in 1886. The reply from Barnsley stated:

> 'Glass Bottle trade; Home trade two thirds. Foreign trade one third. Chiefly to Australia, New Zealand, Cape, South America, India.'

The reply also complained about hostile tariffs and the low price of colonial and foreign produce reflecting the permanent worry of the glassworks owners that the very specialisation which brought their prosperity rendered the industry highly sensitive to any minor shiver in the Victorian economy.

The lock-out of 1893 and opposition to the fixed shift system to be considered in Chapter 7 may have ended in favour of the workers at the time but, as every South Yorkshire glassworks except perhaps Beatson Clark and Redfearns were to find, the next century dealt harshly with any industry that over-specialised unless it was accompanied by heavy capital investment.

CHAPTER 6

20TH CENTURY DECLINE

HISTORY

Perhaps the historian is too close to the events of the present century, especially the inter-war period, to accurately plot the causes of the decline in the nation's glass industry and relate them to the corresponding effect with sufficient clarity. This is particularly the case in Yorkshire as a whole. Although this current research has focused on the South Yorkshire industry it should be noted that the West Yorkshire group of glassworks followed a similar path with even more serious results, being now virtually extinct. South Yorkshire barely survives.

Yet the early years of the century had begun with great flourish. It has been calculated by Hodkin (1953:35) that in the 1930s Yorkshire was producing 28% of all containers made in Britain, it employed over 16% of the nation's glassworkers and output increased 419% compared with the national figure of 312%.

In spite of this, the speed at which works closed can be seen from Figure 20, when the decline may be better described as a collapse. Numerous small works closed but the most serious losses were the major works such as Rylands in 1927, Kilner Brothers in 1939 and Wood Brothers in 1981 together with most Sheffield and Mexborough glassworks.

It will be seen that many factors brought about this collapse but over-specialisation in pursuit of a market brought its own hazards as Rylands discovered when the Codd bottle suddenly went out of fashion in the 1920s in favour of the new screw caps. The firm was totally unable to respond and paid the penalty in its failure to find an alternative market product.

The graph does, however, hide certain important developments. Were it not for the emergence of smaller firms producing a variety of specialist glassware, the rate of descent would have been almost vertical from the 1920s. It is not unlikely, in fact, that there were some short-lived glassworks at the industry's peak which merely processed glass bought in from elsewhere that they themselves had not produced. Recent examples of this method are to be seen at Pilkingtons in Doncaster, set up in the 1930s which processed glass from the St. Helens headquarters and Potters Bellatini, Barnsley, which in the 1960s used Wood's cullet to produce the reflective pellets for road signs. Attempts were made in the inter-war period to revive the industry with new works such as Taylor & Haigh at Owlerton in 1923 and the Sheffield Glass Works in Royds Lane about 1925 but they were of short duration. A new works was set up in 1934 in Doncaster by W.A.Bailey under the Rockware label which, after high hopes, ran into difficulties in the 1960s and has now been subject to a management purchase in 1989. It hopes to continue with a range of coloured glass products.

Another new glassworks founded in 1937 has suffered a similar fate. It was started by Wilfred Barker, then General Manager of Wood Brothers, who left to set up the Waterstone Glasshouse at Wath, taking with him ten 'chairs' to produce crystal glass. After mixed fortunes, including two failures, a recent management purchase has saved it to continue on a small scale as Glastics producing lead crystal cosmetic containers.

The main theme of the century has been closure and reorganisation. In 1902 Wood Brothers decided hand-crafted cut crystal ware was no longer economic and concentrated on high grade medicine and dispensing bottles, feeding bottles and laboratory chemical ware. In 1912 they built a new 12 pot direct-fired furnace which maintained production for the next forty years, but in 1962 they closed the 8 pot works at Wombwell bought in 1901 and tried extensive modernisation of the Hoyle Mill works during the 1950s. Overseas competition and the loss of a major contract with Lucas Industries in 1975 led to a rapid decline, the family firm being bought out by Single Holdings. Continued failure led to a workers' co-operative attempting revival, but in vain. The works went into receivership in February 1981, the last workers were made redundant and the works demolished.

Redfearns, concentrating solely on bottles and jars, enlarged to the point where the Old Mill works was totally inadequate and a new site was acquired in 1946 two miles north-east of Barnsley at Monk

Bretton. The move proved unexpectedly fortuitious as the Barnsley canal burst its banks in November 1946 leaving the Old Mill works isolated without a canal link. This works was demolished and its sole reminder is part of the original canal wharf with barge tie-up rings preserved at the rear of a modern store.

They had also extended in 1930 by absorption of the Fishergate works in York to trade as National Glass but this was closed in the early 1980s and demolished. Under the trading name of Redfearn National Glass the firm survived at its Monk Bretton works and continued to expand through the 1960s and 1970s, eventually producing containers at the rate of three million per day. Despite such expansion the international competition reduced trading profits to the point when, in 1989, it lost its British identity and was bought out by Swedish PLM Industries. The family connection remains in name only as PLM Redfearn Glass.

By planned diversification into a range of glass products Beatson Clark has progressed throughout the present century. After buying the empty site of the defunct Hope (Rylands) works at Stairfoot, Barnsley, in 1929 the firm expanded production though modernisation was slow. At the end of 1929 some 98% of production was mouth-blown and 2% semi-automatic press and blow machines with an output of 1100 gross per week. By 1949 output was 80% fully automatic, 19% semi-automatic and 1% mouth-blown giving a weekly average production of 12,500 gross of bottles. Mouth-blown containers were still being made in 1954. Production continued to grow to an annual bottle output:

1960	163 million
1970	507 million
1980	640 million
1990	565 million (increased bottle size)

It too has now fallen to the recent trend in the financial markets to amalgamate multiple firms under a corporate banner and in 1989 lost its family connections to become part of Tyzack Turner.

In 1902 the firm of P.T.Turner moved from Sussex Street in Sheffield, where it had operated since 1890, to establish a bottle works in Attercliffe, adjacent to the site noted earlier as Sarah Slater's plot, in Darnall Road. It was a short-lived venture, closing in 1922, but was destined to be part of what became an internationally famed organisation when it attracted the attentions of the University of Sheffield which purchased the redundant works in 1924 for research and development as part of the new Department of Glass Technology. After the last war the Department moved to the present building in Northumberland Road, Sheffield, and the Darnall Road site was reduced to waste land.

There is little doubt that glass will continue to play a part in modern life and new uses found for its apparently infinite varieties, such as glass fibre cables for optics and electronic transmissions. But the objects which have become all too familiar as the basic 'bread and butter' of the industry are seriously under threat. Cans are replacing beer bottles, milk and wine are sold in waxed cartons, plastic is used in windows and tumblers are made from plastics – perhaps the future of decorative glass and the wine glass is assured. But the rate of change in the last thirty years exceeds anything that occurred in the previous three hundred and any forecast would be little more than a poor guess.

TECHNOLOGY

Despite the doom and gloom of the massive loss of glassworks suffered in the region during this period, the actual production of glass increased dramatically. The two, of course, were not unrelated and have their roots in the introduction of machines to replace men in addition to the loss of international markets at the turn of the century. Deane (1979:294) comments on

> '..the characteristically low propensity to invest and to innovate which seems to have distinguished British entrepreneurs in the late nineteenth century from their rivals in other industrializing countries'.

Firms which failed to realise the importance of machine production and that the end of mouth blowing was in sight were the first to go under. Unfortunately, even where owners invested in machinery to challenge the markets, they then met the resentment and resistance of the craftsmen the machine was to replace. This, as will be seen in the next chapter, accelerated the decline even further.

The two-man Ashley machine had already begun to make its mark as the new century dawned. Using simple levers the operator could

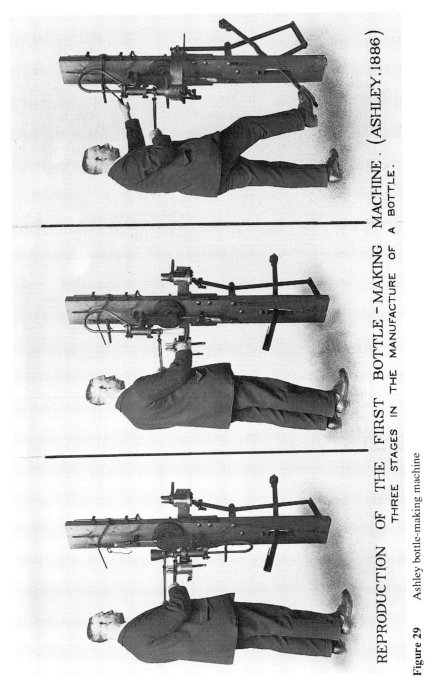

REPRODUCTION OF THE FIRST BOTTLE - MAKING MACHINE. (ASHLEY, 1886)
THREE STAGES IN THE MANUFACTURE OF A BOTTLE.

Figure 29   Ashley bottle-making machine

Figure 30 Owen bottle-making machine

open and close the mould and blow the bottle with compressed air. He only needed an assistant to introduce the gob of glass and remove the finished bottle to the lehr.

By 1907 the first impact of a truly automatic machine was felt throughout the industry. In that year Kilners at Thornhill Lees and Rylands at Stairfoot introduced the Owen, fully automatic, bottle machine. It could extract glass from the tank in correct quantities, dispensing with a gatherer, and with ten rotary mould heads using compressed air blowing, was capable of continuous production at a rate which completely revolutionised the industry. It was a bitter irony that the industry became a victim of its own success as the available markets were rapidly saturated.

Under the chair system which had supplied the needs for over a century a highly skilled team of five workers were expected to produce about 150 bottles an hour. This figure is often quoted in histories of the period but must be treated with some reservation in view of the evidence given by the glassworkers to the Magistrates at a Court inquiry into the Rylands dispute reported in the Barnsley Chronicle of 26 September 1886. Wages for the chair were calculated on a base of 57 dozen (684) bottles in a seven hour shift, about 98 per hour.

> Q. It has been said a workman can make 70 dozen in seven hours?
> A. There are good and bad workmen in our trade: there are workmen who could make 70 dozen.
> Q. Is that the general run of workmen or something exceptional?
> A. Exceptional.
> Q. Is that 70 dozen saleable bottles?
> A. No, they have to be riddled down by sorting after that we... are only paid for what is good and saleable.

From this it is clear that 120 an hour was exceptional and around 100 normal, some of which would be rejected and well short of the owner's hopeful 150.

With the Ashley machine this went up to about 200 perfect bottles but required just two unskilled operators. The fully automatic Owen machine could turn out 2500 bottles an hour virtually unattended. Production at Beatson Clark which had been 13,200 dozen bottles per week mouth-blown became 150,000 dozens per week after automation.

Few records survive to calculate comparative costs but at the Sykes glassworks in Castleford it had been estimated in the early days of automation that each gathering hole under the chair system cost 3s 6d per gross bottles in labour whereas the machine costs per hole equated to 3d per gross labour.

Worker resistance to these changes which threatened the privileged position that the glassmaker enjoyed was more effective than anything the weavers or miners were able to accomplish. The craftsman glassmaker (gaffer) had always been supreme and his personal skills at a premium. His tools were few and primitive – a blowing iron, pontil and shears plus the odd bit of wood and leather had been his stock in trade for over two thousand years. Only when the machine challenged this did it become apparent that the glassmakers had ruled the industry, not the glassworks owner, and the inevitable clash is considered in the next chapter.

CHAPTER 7

THE GLASSWORKERS

IN THE COMMUNITY

Unfortunate it may be but historians cannot avoid the reality that any documentary record of the past will tend to be biased towards the rich and influential. The poor and the workers lacking property or fortune have left precious few records of their existence. Yet no review of a whole industry can afford not to find a place for at least some description of their life and work even though the information must often be found at second hand. This chapter attempts to look into the lives of the glassworkers and their families, particularly during the most traumatic period of its history following the nineteenth century expansion, trying to see their view of the industry as previous chapters have tended to see it from that of the owners and innovators who controlled it.

Perhaps the first question to consider is where they lived. At the early glassworks this presented little difficulty as, for example, at Bolsterstone the two cruck-framed cottages adjacent to the works could accommodate owner and manager with the remaining few workers in nearby cottages. Similarly at Silkstone, the Pilmays lived in the house by the works and the other glassmen in cottages along the village street.

The problem really arises with the introduction of the larger cone type glassworks where thirty or more workers and families had to be found living quarters, particularly as it was essential they live near the works. Throughout the time glass was prepared in crucibles there could be no fixed hours of work and the glassmen had to live within easy reach to begin their working shift, or journey, as and when required. Alfred Dunhill, a gatherer from Kilner Brothers at Conisbrough giving evidence to a Parliamentary Commission of Inquiry[1] in 1865 stated:

'.. they could only start when the founder had metal [glass] ready ... which took .. about 15 hours but could vary an hour. The glassworkers did not report to work at a particular time but rather waited until they were sent for ... We are called for the first journey at about 11.0 Sunday night, for the second at 2.0 or 3.0 A.M. on Tuesday and each following journey begins a few hours later than on the day before but it is very uncertain when you begin. Sometimes I am 18 hours at home before being called'.

The hours might vary but the system was based on the custom of centuries.

At other works the men were expected to turn up at 3.0 A.M. but if the glass was not ready they would be sent home, or if it was poor quality, they would refuse to use it and go home to be recalled later when it was ready. As the men would invariably not hurry to return, perhaps having gone to their pigeon loft or back to bed, the owners grumbled that '.. the men could be two hours late returning'.

The problem was exacerbated by the chair system in that, if one member was missing, the other four could not work and that hole produced no glass. Kilner had tried to force prompt arrival by fixing a maximum eleven and a half hour journey day at the end of which any glass remaining was thrown out as waste. This would mean those arriving late would not have time to make up their piece-rate wage. However, until the introduction of the tank furnace ensured that glass was always available and fixed hours agreed, there was no real solution.

Perhaps Thorpe at Gawber had met the problem in the eighteenth century by building the Skyers Row cottages overlooking his glassworks and reputed to have been glassworkers' cottages, though no records survive to confirm this. Wood Brothers certainly accepted the situation in 1873 having '... found by experience that it was desirable to have some of the men .. living close to the works ... It was therefore decided to build ten Stone fronted cottages near the works'.[2]

This housing was rented to the workers but, in Newcastle, housing was considered part of the wages not only to ensure men lived close by but to also discourage their leaving. (It will be seen later that glassworkers were a notoriously mobile workforce). The Newcastle Broad and Crown Glass Works paid:

'superior workmen 25s with free house & coal

second class 21s with free house & coal

labourers 12s – 14s with free house & coal'

It might be thought possible to see this concentration of glassmen near their own works from the evidence of the nineteenth century Census Returns but in the built-up urban areas a number of works were within what was then considered easy walking distance, say four or five miles, and it cannot be known to which works each recorded glassworker belonged. An exceptional case is the Wood Brothers' works at Worsbrough which, being in a still largely rural area and at least eight miles from the nearest works, shows a distinct enclave in the Dale where terraces of cheap housing developed to accommodate the influx of families in the nineteenth century industrial changes in the parish.

Figure 31 shows weavers concentrated for mutual support to the north as an extension over the boundary from the Barnsley weaving industry, miners near the main colliery for convenience and glassworkers close to the glassworks ready for 'call out'. The only exceptions to the concentration of glassworkers near the works were an eleven year old 'maker' and a sixteen year old 'cutter' living on Worsbrough Common. It is, perhaps, an interesting social comment of the times that none of the workers involved in any of these expanding new industries ever lived within the original old village of Worsbrough itself nor did the owners even live in Worsbrough parish, preferring the attractions of Barnsley town life. The most influential landowner in Worsbrough at the time, W.B.Martin, caused the Sheffield turnpike to be diverted away from the old village where he lived so that it could be isolated and gated to create a park in 1840. Clearly the influx of labourers to the new industries were kept apart and out of sight of the old order.

The arrival of a complete glassmaking force in the 1840s at a somewhat isolated South Yorkshire township raises a problem regarding their origins. Working with glass is a craft requiring many years of training and practice to learn the skills and, whilst apprentices were certainly trained at all the works, Rylands employed 102 in 1886 for example, every owner had an initial problem of finding skilled teams, ready-made, to start up a new works.

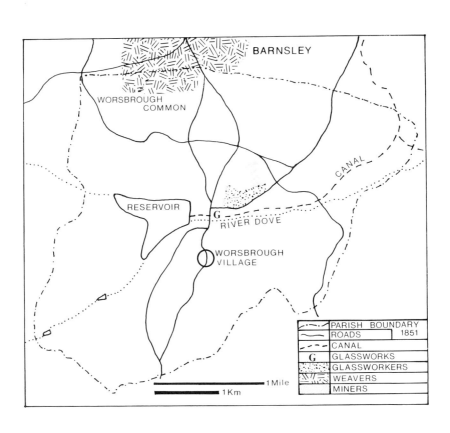

Figure 31   Worsbrough – worker distribution.

106

At Silkstone only five glassworkers can be found to have been there at the start of the eighteenth century yet fifty years later the Darton parish registers show a hundred entries relating to 22 different families of glassworkers at the Gawber works only two miles away.

There was clearly no local pool of skilled men Thorpe could call on but no documentary evidence survives to show from where they were recruited. A similarly frustrating situation faces the researcher at the other glassworks but it has been possible to obtain some indication for the Wood Brothers' works from the Worsbrough Census Returns. The first national Census in 1831 must be discounted as providing no evidence and in 1841 merely indicates if born in Yorkshire or not. But the decennial Censuses from 1851 give valuable information not only for workers' origins but, being relatively isolated from other glassworks, show family relationships to the works and continuity of the craft within the family. It must be recognised, of course, that some workers and their families undoubtedly came and went within the ten year census periods and would not be counted, so absolute totals cannot be obtained.

The Wood Brothers' glassworks was a flint works specialising in cut and engraved glass when founded in 1830. The composition of the workforce can be seen for the period 1841–1881 in Table 1, though it should be noted the works officially closed in 1874 when it moved to Hoyle Mill, Barnsley. The 1881 return suggests some work still carried on at the Worsbrough site, mainly 'finishing-off'. The total workforce was around thirty during its lifetime, which is considered the norm for a cone glassworks as shown by Matsumura (1983:22) from figures relating to Stourbridge.

	Maker	Blower	Cutter	Others	Total
1841	7	8	11	1	27
1851	5	11	14	3	33
1861	6	8	13	6	33
1871	7	7	14	3	31
1881	2	5	5	3	15

Table 1   Workforce composition – Wood Brothers Glassworks.

Family Origin	1851	1861	1871	1881
Hunslet	2	1		
Wakefield	1			
Mirfield	2			
Dudley	4			
Wordsley	1			
Dixons Green	2			
Stourbridge		1		
Staffordshire	1	1		
Worcester	1			
Haughton (Manchester)	2			
Newcastle			1	
Hull	1			
Tilney (Kings Lynn)	1			
Durham	1	1		
Sheffield	1		1	
Oldham	1			
France	1			
York		1		
Birmingham		1		
Worksop		1		
St. Helens		1	3	
St. Albans				1
Mexborough				1
Darfield		1		1
Barnsley		1	2	

Table 2   Employees place of origin – Wood Brothers Glassworks.

The Census fails to distinguish 'gatherers' and it is assumed the 'blowers' did their own gathering. Under 'Others' are included Warehousemen and Labourers.

It can be seen that 90% of the workers were highly skilled men, none of whom could initially be recruited locally. However, as noted in the earlier description of this works in Chapter 5, the Wood brothers were skilled cutters and gilders from the Midlands and Table 2 shows that in 1851 they recruited 40% from this area where they had themselves been employed and 25% from the Lancashire area once known to the Pilmays.

The need to recruit from further afield decreased as local workers acquired the skills, particularly in the case of blowers as shown in Table 3.

	Maker	*Blower*	*Cutter*	*Others*	*Total*
1841	4	6	7	0	17
1851	3	4	8	0	15
1861	4	2	7	2	15
1871	2	0	3	1	6
1881	0	1	1	1	3

Table 3   External recruitment – Wood Brothers Glassworks.

Specialist items, however, could still be a problem even as late as 1914, when they had to recruit three Belgian glass blowers to make light bulbs.

A significant finding from the Census and Parish records is the degree of migration of the glassworkers. Certainly a few families stayed at the Wood Brothers' works for two or three generations but the main emphasis was on movement. For example, two families stayed over a fifty year period but fifty two families appeared on only one Census return then moved on. Of the original seventeen incomers for 1841, ten had left by 1851.

The itinerant way of life of these glassworkers during the period of industrial expansion shown in these statistics is well illustrated by James Slator, for example, who was born in Liverpool in 1825, worked first as a glass cutter in St. Helens (Pilkingtons), moved to Swinton in 1858 and was at Wood Brothers from 1862.

More extreme cases were not uncommon as seen in the evidence given by Matthew Lowe to the Barnsley Magistrates in 1886 during the Rylands (Hope Works) dispute referred to previously. He was born in Cudworth, near Barnsley, had worked at glassworks in Bristol, Castleford, Mexborough and Swinton before arriving at Rylands. Yet he was only 32 years old. At the same inquiry John James had '.. been in the bottle trade 23 years ... in Yorkshire, Lancashire and Gloucestershire; at some places two or three times..'

Despite this constant movement within the industry, it is clear that a strong family tradition of glassmaking persisted. Of the families that could be traced in the late nineteenth century at Wood Brothers, 19 fathers had 25 sons and 2 daughters followed them into the works and only 5 sons chose an alternative (four mining and one wheelwright).

It has been suggested by Matsumura (1983:64) in his analysis of the industry that this migration pattern, particularly from the Midlands, was related to promotion prospects but from the evidence

Figure 32   Glassblower.

at Wood Brothers, between 1841 and 1881, there were only two blowers elevated to 'maker' (gaffer) and none were promoted to cutters. One maker, in fact, was demoted to warehouseman. The reasons for migrations to other glassmaking areas are still unclear and may be nothing more than the hope that it must be better somewhere else.

IN THE GLASSWORKS

Although reliable rates of pay for glassworkers in the early period are not available, some of the problems associated with the employer/employee disputes of the nineteenth century illustrate the practices in arriving at pay rates which had always been peculiar to glassmaking. Over the centuries it had become common for the 'chair' to decide what was a reasonable quantity to produce during a journey (the name given to the normal working day) and on this the basic payment to the whole team was agreed. It then had to be shared differentially according to status in the team. In the early seventeenth century a team making drinking glasses could earn £5 reckoned at a third of the glass value produced which was normally shared between three workers. The founder could earn 7s a week and the teaser 5s. (Average wages for skilled carpenters and masons at the time were about 6s a week).(Godfrey 1975:190)

Payment based on the 'third value' was general whilst the owner was the glassmaker, as in the case of the Pilmays, but had been phased out by the time of the eighteenth century cone works in favour of payment based on what the owner considered a fair return for his invested capital in production costs. But old practices died hard and the chair still decided what they thought was a reasonable quantity to produce during a journey and tried to dictate the payment per item depending on the nature of the product.

A journey was usually considered to be about a seven hour shift early in the nineteenth century, but the team could often continue another three or four hours for over-pay if metal remained, though a movement to an eleven and a half hour shift was common by the end of the century. These hours varied considerably in the different glassmaking regions and were a ready-made source of friction.

The wages structure which evolved during the century was extremely complex and barely understood even by the owners judging from the comments of Alan Clark (then Chairman of Beatson Clark) in his history of the Company (Clark 1980:25).

In a bottle works, for example, an agreement was first reached between management and chair on the number and type of bottles to be produced in a particular time; this became the 'move' and depended on weight, number and quality of product on which payment to the chair was based. Anything produced in excess of this number was rewarded at a higher rate of pay called 'over pay'. A full working day, the journey, might consist of three or four moves as each move could have been producing different kinds of bottle which attracted different rates of pay. At some works a chair would be allowed to use up any glass remaining in the crucible at the end of the journey, often by apprentices to experiment and practice by making 'friggers' which could be fantastic shapes or models or simply the ubiquitous glass walking stick. From the Beatson Regulations (Figure 33) the latter was clearly to be discouraged at the Rotherham Glassworks.

Such a payment system involving individual moves, quantities, qualities and a time element which permitted over pay was an inevitable source of friction. The owner would prefer a longer 'set' period and reduce over pay; the glassworkers sought a shorter set and smaller move to increase the chance of over pay. Owners tried various methods to reduce the over pay – when Kilner's men increased the limit to £2 they were locked out. He brought in unemployed glassworkers and won the dispute. An alternative ploy was to reduce the chair payment which, although it had to be agreed with the men, usually resulted in increased production as they tried to make sufficient to keep up their wages. The extract from the Wood Brothers' accounts (Figure 34) gives new reduced rates for the press shop[3] introduced in 1875.

Further complications arose with the Flint glass workers who considered themselves superior to common bottle men and were able to negotiate higher rates per move.

Any comparison of rates over a period of time or even between individual works is clearly impossible under such a system of wages calculation when the rate for the same product could vary almost daily but examples of average pay provide some indication.

NOTICE.

Workmen are strictly prohibited using the Metal for any other purpose than making their Work.

Anyone found making, or carrying off the Premises, Glass Walking Sticks, or other Fancy Articles, Bottles, &c., &c., without having first obtained permission, will be punished.

BEATSON & Co.

Rotherham Glass Works, 1st March, 1871.

ANN HINCHLIFFE & SON, PRINTERS, &c., ROTHERHAM.

Figure 33   Works notice – Beatson & Co. 1871

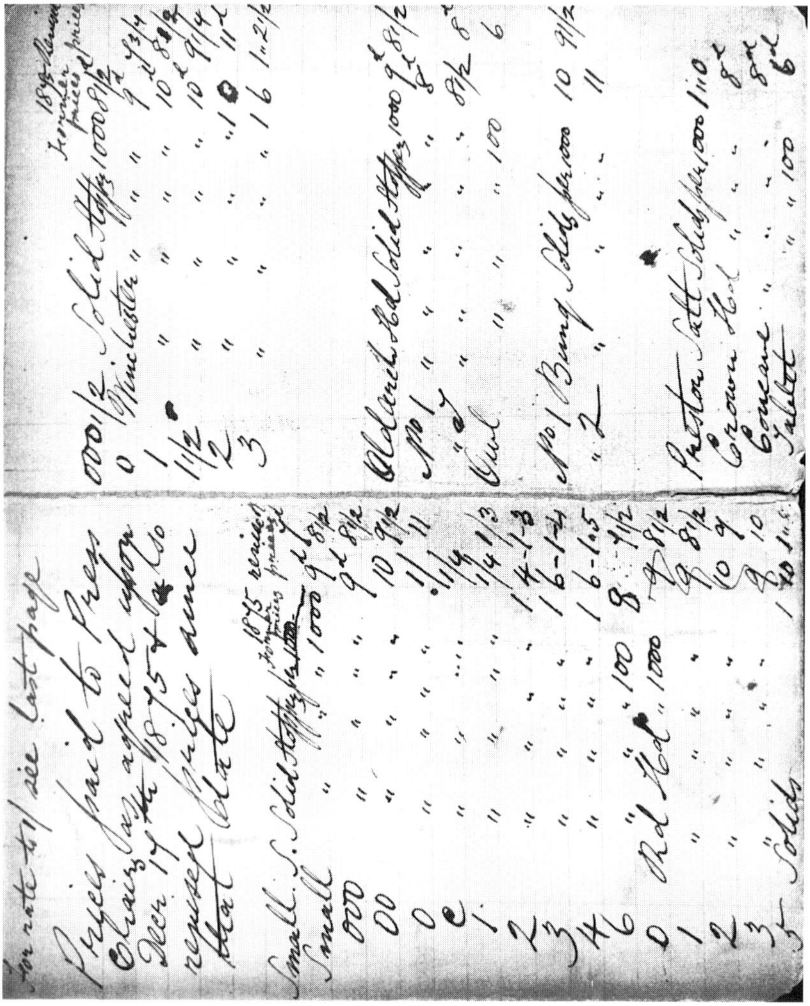

For rate to 1/ see last page

Prices paid to Press Chairs as agreed upon Decr 17th 1875 & also revised prices since that date

		1875 former prices	revised prices
Small S. Solid Stoppers per 1000			
Small	" " " 1000	9d	8½
000	" " " "	9d	8½
00	" " " "	10	9½
0	" " " "	1/	11
C	" " " "	1/4	
1	" " " "	1/4	1/3
2	" " " "	1.4	1-3
3	" " " "	1.6	1-4
4	" " " "	1.6	1.5
6	" " 100	8	7½
0	Rd Hd " 1000	9	8½
1	" " " "	9	8½
2	" " " "	10	9
3	" " " "	9	10
5	Solids	1 10	1.5

		18 former prices	Revised prices
000½	Solid Stoppers 1000	8½d	
0	Winchester " " "	9d	8¾
1	" " " "	10d	8½
1½	" " " "	10d	9¼
2	" " " "	1	11d
3	" " " "	1 6	1.2½
Oldarch Hd Solid Stoppers 1000		9d	8½
No 1	" " " "	8d	
" 2	" " " "	8½	8d
Oval	" " " 100		6
No 1 Bung Solids per 1000		10	9½
" 2	" " "	11	
Preston Salt Solids per 1000		1.10	
Crown Hd	" " "	8d	
Concave	" " "	8d	
Tablet	" " 100	6d	

Figure 34 Work rate agreement – Wood Brothers 1875

In 1841 at a Stourbridge Flint works the average weekly pay was 57s to the chair which was shared according to seniority, including sliding-scale over pay:

Gaffer	28s	+	2s over
Servitor	16s	+	1s over
Footmaker	9s	+	10d over
Taker-in	4s	+	10d over

(These wages might appear reasonable in comparison to other workers as, for example, a Newcastle colliery in the same year was paying a miner 20s and a boy of eleven pulling tubs 5s a week. An agricultural worker earned between 18s and 20s a week).

At Beatson Clark the flint workers could not even agree between themselves and in 1908 the wages book shows payments to:

The New Flint House

> £2 – 19s – 10d
> £2 – 12s – 2d
> £1 – 5s – 0d
> 9s – 8d

The Old Flint House

> £1 – 13s – 8d
> £1 – 6s – 8d
> £1 – 1s – 8d
> 5s – 9d

(The book fails to distinguish the actual job specification but would approximately follow that of the Stourbridge example).

In 1886 the Yorkshire Bottle Works owners assumed a set rate of 63 dozen bottles a day journey (756 a week) based on a seven and a half hour shift to earn:

Gaffer	30s (Over pay was 5s a gross
Blower	28s large and 4s 6d small bottles)
Gatherer	23s
Wetter-off	9s (boys)
Taker-in	8s (boys)

A typical agreement of 1895 shows the various quantities to be made by the chair depending on bottle size (Figure 35).

By 1908 the Beatson Clark rates had increased to;

> Maker (gaffer)   33s 6d + 2s 5d over
> Blower   29s 6d + 2s 1d over

This was based on fourteen moves a week but if less were completed the men had to pay back the equivalent cost of lost production!

Problems continually disrupted relations between employer /employee when glass was not ready or a furnace had to be rebuilt. The latter case was detailed in the 1886 dispute at Rylands when, after closing a furnace, he shared the men amongst the other furnaces and divided them into three sets to work three shifts of seven hours instead of two at ten and a half. The men objected there would not be time to produce enough bottles to make up their standard wage and first suggested he sack the men from the faulty furnace. He refused and the workforce went on strike. Rylands claimed the right 'without any disrespect or defiance to his workpeople, to regulate what use he should make of his premises ... and declined to be dictated to as to whom he should employ.' It had traditionally been agreed in the bottle trade that masters could regulate hours.

He took a test case to the Magistrate's Court (Barnsley Chronicle; 25 September 1886) to claim damages from a workman, James Lindley, to a total of 8s 2d for each shift lost. It comprised:

> 2s 2d   fuel cost
> 6d   furnace maintenance
> 7d   wear & tear
> 2d   management cost
> 2s 2d   2 apprentice wages (his share)
> 2s 6d   cost share 5 gross bottle production lost

Rylands lost the case because the Magistrates felt that, although three shift operations had already been adopted at some works and even sharing holes had become common practice, he had not given the men a week's notice of the change.

The case illustrates the entrenched positions of owner and men which by mid-nineteenth century had led to the formation of societies to protect their interests. Around 1838 the 'Glass Bottle Makers of Yorkshire United Trade Protection Society' had been formed by the men together with an alternative Flint Makers Association. The owners formed their own protection societies, the 'Yorkshire Glass

FLINT GLASS BOTTLE MAKERS'
CATALOGUE

Of Numbers of Articles to be made per move as agreed between Masters and Men for the County of Yorkshire,

JULY 1st, 1895.

STANDARD LIST.

The Numbers for Coloured are taken as Basis for the other two classes of Metal as follows—

The Numbers for Hard White: similar to Coloured to 2 oz., 20 less to 12 oz., and 10 less for the remainder.

The Numbers for Flint: similar to Hard White to 4 oz., 20 less to 12 oz., and 10 less for the remainder.

	2 oz.	4 oz.	6 oz.	8 oz.	10 oz.	12 oz.	16 oz.	20 oz.	24 oz.	32 oz.	40 oz.	50 oz.
Coloured	340	340	320	300	280	260	220	200	180	160	140	120
Hard White	340	320	300	280	260	240	210	190	170	150	130	110
Flint ..	340	320	280	260	240	220	200	180	160	140	120	100

NOTE.—The term Coloured is confined to Coloured Glass without Lead.

Do. Hard White is confined to Colourless Glass without Lead.

Do. Flint includes Coloured and Colourless Glass with Lead.

Figure 35   Standard production list for Yorkshire 1895.

117

Bottle Manufacturers Association' in 1876 and the flint glass owners their own 'Yorkshire Flint Glass Manufacturers Association' by 1891.

An early effect of the rival claims of these organisations was a move by the owners to refuse employment to workers who were union members (Rylands paid 1s a week extra to non-union workers, withdrawn if they later joined). A prime mover in the formation of these unions was the drive by owners to introduce a six journey week to replace the long accepted five. Ultimately the disagreement on this and a variety of wages problems beginning to emerge as machinery was introduced led to the national lock-out in 1893. A least one works, Dobson & Nalls of Barnsley, refused to join the lock-out but the disruption was a major cause of the rapid decline of the industry as foreign competition took over local markets and export markets were lost during the closure.

The owners sought to (a) reduce wages, (b) remove workshare at holes, (c) limit apprentices, (d) not pay men for reject bottles even if not their fault (particularly the 'flown marble' problem where a defective marble stuck in the bottle).

The men won the battle and the established practices were restored; but they lost the war as manufacturers were driven further toward mechanisation, despite a rule made by the men's Union that 'Bottle making machines shall not be put into the bottle house amongst the bottle hands, and members shall not be displaced by machines'. (Hodkin 1953:27).

The complexities of the wages structure which combined varying hours for set work and overplus pay; varying quantities expected to be produced during both; limits on overpay; different rates per product and graduations of differential between those making up a chair (complicated in all cases by distinctions between flint and bottle makers) meant that at no time in the industry could any national pay scales be agreed. Perhaps this was a major factor in the mobility of the workforce, seeking to find a works which offered what best suited individual aspirations.

Against the workers' search for a reasonable living was the owners' desperate struggle to keep an assured market. One of the first meetings of the Manufacturers Association fixed the prices they were to charge to avoid a price war and even agreed a 10% surcharge for goods sold on the London market.

Profits were a sole consideration, often to be maintained by arbitrarily reducing the payments to the men as in 1877 when a 3s cut in wages was imposed and a 6s cut in 1879. A strike and lock-out ensued which ended when the men accepted a 3s reduction. In 1887 overplus rates were cut which encouraged increased production rates as men were forced to make extra to bring up their pay. Nor were the workers helped by their fragmented Union structure as seen at Wood Brothers where there was constant friction betweeen mouth-blowers and machine men because the former had 2s per week extra.

Even the aristocracy of the industry, the engravers and grinders, were not immune. Since the beginning of glass engraving, the motive power for the cutting disc had been supplied by a small boy turning a wheel. The cutter paid his wages but, when owners provided water or steam power, the cutter had to pay the owner back the equivalent of the boy's wages which could be up to a third of his own wages.[4]

Modern terminology such as 'job satisfaction' or 'pride in craftsmanship' would be unheard of amongst the early glassmakers and probably denied by the nineteenth century workers struggling to survive on uncertain wages. Yet some such deep, perhaps unrecognised, motivation has to be invoked together with kinship ties when the actual working conditions are considered for the industry to have thrived at all when a living wage was a daily struggle for survival.

The heat, particularly in the small early glassworks and the cones, was the main concern. The Report of the Commission on Employment of Children in 1843 states that

> 'In Mr.Rice Harris's glasshouse, Birmingham, at the mouth of the lehr, where the boys put in the glass articles, the temperature is 137° F [58° C]; while at the mouth of the furnace where the metal is taken out the temperature is 200° F [93° C]. The men's clothes are frequently scorched during their work, and every solid substance within the range of distance from the furnace mentioned [18–20 ft] will instantly burn the hand'.

To gain respite from this heat it is to be expected the workers resorted to drink. The Manchester Guardian of 3 June 1868 reporting on the first TUC congress quoted a union representative; 'Drink was as great an enemy to the glass bottle maker as the worst employer who ever lived.'

The owners also recognised the effects of drinking on output and tried to curb it by heavy penalties. The Wood Brothers' Manager's Day Book[5] for the 1890s records numerous infringements, for example:

16 March 1891 — William Moss was cautioned about sending for beer into the shop.
18 March 1891 — was fined 5s for same.
16 June 1890 — A. Hobson neglected his work through beer and was fined 5s.
— W.Taylor neglected his work through beer and was fined 5s.

Although such fines represented about a fifth of a week's wages they were clearly not effective as repeated entries show. W.Taylor was again fined 5s on 14 July for sending for beer when at work.

The men also received little sympathy from the Commission of Inquiry in 1843 which considered the effects of working near the heat of the furnace. Somewhat heartlessly, it reported that,

'Evaporation goes on most rapidly; and this evaporation is the cooling process ... Hence the human body is not only capable of bearing exposure to these high temperatures with impunity, but even of pursuing a laborious occupation in them. From every pore of the skin on the exterior, and from the whole surface of the lungs on the interior, an aqueous fluid is poured out most copiously...'.

No mention is made of how to replace this loss of 'aqueous fluid'.

Children employed in the glassworks were particularly affected by the heat. In 1851 Wood Brothers had two girls and three boys under ten years old, including a blower despite the 1843 recommendation that it was

'.. questionable whether boys are not permitted to the duty of glass blowing at much too young an age.'

The Report continued that,

'The temperature of glasshouses is .. extreme .. the heat of furnaces naturally produces rushing draughts and children are exposed to extremes of temperature, suffer colds, rheumatic affections and nausea and vomiting ... The heat affects the sight of the boys'.

One boy told the Commissioners the heat made his eyes sore and bloodshot and

'... was nearly blind for seven weeks, could only see a wee bit'.

The eyesight of the adult gatherers was also of concern as their day was spent looking directly into the white heat of the furnace to gather glass from the crucible and glaucoma was a common ailment. A blower reported that

'... the present work is tiresome and bad for the health ... pains in the breast ... sometimes has turned dizzy with exhaustion of blowing ... a little swelling behind the ear'.

A boy of 13 reported he had been a blower for a year and earned 4s a week blowing about 250 bottles.

'He got heartburn once a week or so – he put a small piece of coal in his cheek and sucks it, he does not feel the heartburn'.

Hernias, skin diseases and chest infections from the dust were all common dangers to the glassworker in the furnace area. The glass cutters, however, escaped these problems only to encounter their own, even more dangerous, health risks with lung diseases caused by the fine silica dust generated in grinding. The boy assisting the grinder ran a greater risk still – he stood over the spinning disc feeding it with 'dry putty powder' as the cutting agent which consisted of three parts lead and one of tin.

He constantly inhaled this toxic mixture as he fed the wheel and, unless he washed his hands carefully before eating, would ingest some in addition. As no time off was allowed for meals and they '.. got their victuals as they could.. ', hygiene probably had a low priority.

That the glassworkers survived at all in these conditions to create one of the region's major industries is remarkable but many are known to have still been active workers into their seventies. Moreover, they must surely, in a perverse way, have enjoyed it and perhaps the last word should be from Matthew Linn who had told the Commission he wished for no other job than to be in a glassworks.

RULES

AND

REGULATIONS

TO BE OBSERVED BY THOSE EMPLOYED AT THE

ROTHERHAM GLASS WORKS.

1. Any Person omitting to come to work at the proper time, or who, after having come, shall absent himself, or neglect his work, will be held liable for any loss or damage thereby occasioned, and to be prosecuted in the Magistrates' Court where necessary.

2. Any Person entering the Works within Ten Minutes after the Bell has ceased ringing, will be allowed Full time; if not more than Forty Minutes after will have Half-an-hour taken off; after Forty minutes no person will be allowed to enter until the next time appointed for commencing work.   It is to be understood that punctuality is expected.

3. Notice will be given and required in the different departments as under :

4. Flint hands, Flint-house Teazers, Lear-men, Flint and Bottle Metal Mixers, Mould-makers Blacksmiths, Stopperers and Glass-cutters, Pot-makers and Clay-men.---Twenty-eight days' notice.'

5. Bottle hands, Founders, Teazers and Cave-men, also Boys employed in Bottle-houses--- A week's notice.

6. All Persons employed in Warehouses, Yard-men who have been in our employ Three Months.---A Fortnight's notice.   Other Yard-men no notice.

7. No Person will be allowed to enter or leave the Works by any other than the principal entrance, at which the Lodge Keeper is stationed.

8. Any Person unable to come to work, through sickness or otherwise, must send notice to that effect, and if required, a medical certificate, to the Manager.

9. FIGHTING, SWEARING, and DISTURBANCES of any kind are strictly prohibited.

10. SMOKING in Warehouses is strictly prohibited.

11. Every precaution must be taken to guard against Fire.

12. Any Person Breaking Windows through carelessness, will have to pay the amount of damage done, or Throwing Stones, &c., will be liable to a Shilling Fine.

13. No Person will be allowed to introduce any Stranger into the Works without permission from the Office.

14. All Persons are strictly prohibited using the Metal for any other purpose than making their Work. Anyone found making or carrying off the premises, Glass Walking Sticks, Fancy Articles, Bottles, &c., &c., without having first obtained permission, will be punished.

BEATSON AND CO.

June 22nd, 1874

Figure 36   Works regulations – Beatson & Co. 1874.

122

The Commissioners wrote,

> 'He calls himself 12 but looks about 10. Takes in bottles to the arch. Has been doing this a year – was at a mill treading clay for half a year – has been about two and a half years working atdifferent things – once had a sore throat and once was very sick ... has forgotten most of his learning now.'

With his stamina and commitment he could look forward to promotion as gaffer or even set up his own works as many had done before him. Unfortunately his ultimate fate has gone unrecorded but his like can never be forgotten in the creation (and perhaps decline) of the industry. Though science and technology have replaced gaffer, gatherer and blower the memory of his heyday lives on in the many families involved in the region's once great industry and has a symbolic reminder as a supporter on the Barnsley civic coat of arms.

A commercial glass industry has existed in South Yorkshire for nearly four hundred years. In that time it may not have achieved international acclaim with a superlative product such as the Newcastle baluster or the St.Helens plate glass, though possibly can lay claim to the style of tableware ascribed to Nailsea. Perhaps its reputation may linger in the oddity of its world-conquering Codd bottle.

History would be unkind, however, simply to recall South Yorkshire as the home of the bottle – it should also be remembered for its contribution to the early advances in the new coal fuel technology, the inventive genius of men such as Rylands and the army of glassworkers who produced a variety of glassware to a consistent high quality whether for rich table or poor ale house.

Despite the continuing challenge of new materials glassmaking in the area survives into this new age, even though on a reduced scale, and the history of the South Yorkshire glass industry has not ended.

SOUTH YORKSHIRE GLASSWORKS GAZETTEER

i) Section A lists all glassworks known to have made glass and are in alphabetical order by location of nearest town/village and civil parish. Unless otherwise stated, no trace of the works now survives and the sites are not open to the public.

ii) Section B lists works occasionally given in Trade Directories etc. as 'manufacturers' but were cutters and grinders of products from flint glassworks.

iii) Section C lists 'manufacturers' in Directories where the address given refers to offices or warehouse, not a glassmaking site.

iv) Entries marked (Tr.Dir.) contain Trade Directory dates though works often continued beyond the final date given.

v) Entries marked * are tentative, present evidence inconclusive.

vi) O.S. Map reference is 1:10560 series; street address is given where actual site of building cannot be identified.

SECTION A – GLASSWORKS

1. Barnsley; Dobson & Nalls. (SE/359063). 1881–1920s. Bottle works. Reported in Mexborough & Swinton Times of 6 January 1893 as the only local firm not joining in national lock-out during bottle-makers' strike.

2. Barnsley; Gawber I. (SE/327076). c.1700. Lead glass. Excavation report of furnace remains in Ashurst.D., Post Medieval Archaeology, (1970), Vol.4, pp.92–140. Dated thermo-remanent magnetic survey, Oxford Research Laboratory.

3. Barnsley; Gawber II. (SE/327076). 1734–1824. Bottle and window glass. Built and owned by Thorpe family. Brick cone furnace demolished 1824 and ground cleared for agriculture. Built over by housing estate in 1980s. Excavation report as Gawber I (see No.2). Finds in Sheffield City Museum.

4. Barnsley; Guest. c.1875. (Tr.Dir.). Bottles.

5. Barnsley; Manor Flint Glass Works, Stairfoot. (SE/375054). 1895–1938. (Tr.Dir.) Tomlinson owners producing marbles for Rylands and tableware. Site now destroyed.

6. Barnsley; Oaks Glass Bottle Works. (SE/368061). 1872–1927. Owners Sutcliffe, Wade & Dobson. Modified 'Codd' bottle invented by Sutcliffe 1878. Site now destroyed.

7. Barnsley; Old Mill. (SE/351069) 1861–1946 and Monk Bretton (SE/373084) 1946–Present. Bottles and containers. Original works by James Wragg bought and extended by J. & S. Redfearn brothers in 1862. Took over additional works at Aldham Bridge works, Wombwell, from 1895 to early 1900s and Fishergate Glassworks, York, (closed 1980s). Old Mill works trading as Redfearn Brothers closed and demolished in 1946 and new site established at Monk Bretton as Redfearn National Glass. Now trading as PLM Redfearn Glass.

8. Barnsley; Potters Bellatini, Hoyle Mill. (SE/359062). 1960–Present. Reflective glass beads for road signs. Originally used cullet from adjacent Wood Brothers, Hoyle Mill, works.

9. Barnsley; Hope Glass Works, Stairfoot. (SE/375053). 1867–1927. Bottles and containers. Founded by Ben Rylands and succeeded by son Dan responsible for many innovations in 19th century bottle-making technology. Works closed in 1927 and empty site purchased by Beatson Clark of Masbrough to build bottle works. Currently in production as Beatson Clark. (See No.24).

10. Barnsley; Wood Brothers, Hoyle Mill. (SE/359063). (See No. 63, Worsbrough).

11. Catcliffe, Rotherham. (SK/425887). 1740–1884 (Possibly re-used briefly 1901). Bottles, flint & window glass. Built by William Fenney from Bolsterstone (see No.50). Series of subsequent owners, May, Blunn & Booth and Greenfield & Jones. Brick cone survives, preserved as ancient monument.

Free public access. Unpublished excavation 1962 by Sheffield Museum.

12. Conisbrough, Doncaster; Providence Glass Works. (SK/504997). 1844–1939. Bottles and jars. Works founded by Kilner Brothers as addition to main works at Thornhill Lees and Castleford (West Yorkshire).

13. Doncaster; Pilkington. 1930s to present. Glass processed from main works at St. Helens, Lancashire.

14. Doncaster; Rockware. 1934–Present. W.A.Bailey owner. Small domestic items, flint glass, plain & coloured.

15. Kilnhurst, Rotherham; Hardy Son & Saxton. 1901–1905. (Tr.Dir).

16. Kilnhurst, Rotherham; Saxton. C.1901. (Tr.Dir.) Additional to No.15 above.

17. Kilnhurst, Rotherham; Victoria Works. 1856–1895. Bottle works. Owner Blunn. (Tr.Dir.).

18. Mexborough, Rotherham; Bach & Nevill. 1845–1850. (Tr.Dir.).

19. Mexborough, Rotherham; Bull Green. (SE/488005). 1879–1893. Bottle works. Owner Barron Hartley then John Lowe. (Tr.Dir.) Possibly two separate works ie. 1879–1883 then 1881–1893).

20. Mexborough, Rotherham; Don Works. 1842. Founder Micklethwaite then George Bach to 1849. (Tr.Dir.).

21. Mexborough, Rotherham; Don Works. (SK/472997). 1850–1905. Bottle works. Unknown owner until Joseph Barron in 1905. Possibly same works as No.20.

22. Mexborough, Rotherham; New Don Works. (SK/469997). 1857–1920. Bottle works. Owner J.Barron to 1897 then

P.Waddington, previously a partner, and his successors to 1920 closure.

23. Mexborough, Rotherham; Phoenix. (SK/471997. 1876–1989. Owners Barron family. Thomas Barron returned to 'old Don Works' and renamed it Phoenix. Available documents confuse the works Nos. 21, 22 and 23. Phoenix alternatively called Mexborough Flint Glass Works in 1850 and Nos. 21 and 23 were adjacent.

24. Rotherham; Beatson Clark, Masbrough. (SK/425934) 1751–Present. Bottle, flint and window glass, later concentrating on medical and chemical ware. Cones built by John Wright & Partners, bought by John Beatson in 1783 and by marriage became known as Beatson Clark. Expanded throughout 19th and 20th centuries, last cone demolished 1945. Expanded by purchase of site of redundant Rylands works (Hope Glass Works, No.9) in 1929. Firm currently trades under Beatson Clark label but owned by Tyzack Turner from 1989.

25. Rotherham; Langwell. 1901. (Tr.Dir.).

26. Rotherham; Morgan. 1881–1901. (Tr.Dir.).

27. Rotherham; New York Bottle House, Brinsworth. 1860–? (Tr.Dir.).

28. Rotherham; Platts. 1893–? (Tr.Dir.).

29. Rotherham; Templeborough. (SK/413916) Roman 1st cent. A.D. Archaeological evidence of glassworking in workshop outside Roman fort in civil settlement.

30. Sheffield; Attercliffe, Darnall Road. (SK/384886). c.1775–c.1850. Bottle glassworks. Advertised 1793 under J.Dixon. Occupied by Carr on Fairbank 1819 survey which shows cone glassworks. Site presently under Sanderson Kayser steelworks.

31. Sheffield; Attercliffe. * Don Flint & Green Works. 1850–1859. Melling Carr & Co. (Tr.Dir.).

32. Sheffield; Attercliffe. * Langwell & Co. 1876–1879. (Tr.Dir.).

33. Sheffield; Attercliffe. * William Langwell 1883. (Tr.Dir.). Note: Insufficient evidence to determine if 31, 32 and 33 are distinct or same works under new partners.

34. Sheffield; Don Glass Works, Darnall Road, (SK/385885). 1850–1972?) Built by Melling Carr, taken over by Mycock 1861 then Langwell 1872. Moved to Cleveland Square in 1870s as Langwell Brothers trading under 'Don Works' label. Flint glass.

35. Sheffield; Langwell & Co., Darnall Road. 1898. Flint and bottle works. (Tr.Dir.). Possibly site as No.34 under changed trade name.

36. Sheffield; Gunstone & Co., Stevenson Road. 1897–1901. Bottle works. (Tr.Dir.).

37. Sheffield; Langwell Bros., Joiner Street. 1898. Flint glass. (Tr.Dir.).

38. Sheffield; Langwell Bros., Stanley Street. 1898–1905. Flint glass. (Tr.Dir.).

39. Sheffield; Mellowes & Co., Corporation Street. 1888–1893. Flint glass. (Tr.Dir.).

40. Sheffield; Thomas Mycock, Carlton Road. * 1862. (Tr.Dir.).

41. Sheffield; Primrose & Co., Corporation Street. 1872–1883. Flint glass. (Tr.Dir.).

42. Sheffield; Robert Langwell, Saxon Road. 1920/1. Bottle works. (Tr.Dir.).

43.   Sheffield; Taylor Haigh, Bradfield Road, Owlerton. *
       1923–1925.(Tr.Dir.).

44.   Sheffield; Palm Tree * 1892–1900 (Tr.Dir.).

45.   Sheffield; John Turner & Co. 1856. (Tr.Dir.).

46.   Sheffield; P.T.Turner & Co., Sussex Street 1856–1903,
       moved to Darnall Road 1902–1922.(SK/384886). Bottle
       works. Purchased in 1924 by Department of Glass
       Technology, Sheffield University. Department moved to
       Northumberland Road in 1950s, Darnall Road site cleared.
       Currently waste land.

47.   Sheffield; J.W. Ward, Bressingham Road. 1893. Bottle works.
       (Tr.Dir.).

48.   Sheffield Glass Works, Royds Lane, 1925.

49.   Silkstone, Barnsley; SE/293058). c.1650–1710/20. Bottles,
       window and flint glass (plain and coloured). Ground leased
       by William Scott to John & Peter Pilmay, descendants of 16c.
       French immigrants. John married Abigail, widow of son of
       William Scott. Abigail joined William Clifton of Glass
       Houghton in petition to Parliament against Glass Tax. Scotts
       continued glassmaking after death of Pilmays to c.1710/20
       then converted to a pottery site. Francis Morton, glassmaker
       with the Pilmays transferred to Gawber II then Castleford.

50.   Stocksbridge; Bolsterstone, Sheffield; (SK/266980).
       c.1650–1758. Bottle, window and lead flint. Owned by Fox
       family and Robert Blackburn by marriage. Glassmaker
       William Fenney (see Catcliffe, No.11). Unique furnace
       producing wide range of decorative tableware and household
       articles. Site converted to pottery 1770–1796. Building
       preserved as ancient monument, access by arrangement.
       Excavation report Ashurst.D., (1987) Post Medieval
       Archaeology, Vol.21, 147–226. Finds in Sheffield City
       Museum.

51. Swinton; Dale Brown, Rotherham. * 1920–1925. Bottle works. Dale Brown began operating a glassworks in 1913 which had been derelict and may be this site. (Tr.Dir.).

52. Swinton; South Yorkshire Glass Company, Rotherham; * (SK/4699) 1852–present. Originally Swinton Glassworks changed name in 1933 to Dale Brown and in 1962 to Canning Town Glass. Post 1958 took over site of adjacent iron foundry creating two glassworks. Currently trading as United Glass Containers. (Tr.Dir.).

53. Wath; Comer Brothers. 1877–1930s. (Tr.Dir.).

54. Wath; Strafford. 188–? (Tr.Dir.).

55. Wath; Waterstone. 1937–1960. Flint lead glass. Wilfred Barker set up works after leaving Wood Brothers (see No.63) from Hoyle Mill. Renamed Glastics in 1960s which continues small-scale production of lead glass cosmetic containers.

56. Wentworth, Rotherham. (SK/397985). 1632–1642. Window glass. Ground leased by Earl of Strafford, (beheaded 1641), financed by Sir Robert Mansell. Glassmaker Francis Bristow, related to Bungar family of 16c. immigrants, imprisoned 1642 for non-payment of monopoly dues to Mansell.

57. Wombwell; Aldham Bridge. * 1870s. Dickinson & Hammerton owners. Recorded in Jessop (Worsbrough) Lime Kiln accounts–possibly a related but separate works from No. 58.

58. Wombwell; Aldham Bridge. 1872–1895 (–1901 ?). Dickinson owner until taken over by Redfearn Brothers in 1895. Closure date unknown but about 1901.

59. Wombwell; Dearne & Dove. (SE/401032). 1872–1927. When referred to as 'Lister bottle works' became subsidiary of Rylands–end of lease unknown.

60. Wombwell; Lowe. c.1879. Bottle works. (Tr.Dir.).

61.   Wombwell; Moore. c.1879. Bottle works. (Tr.Dir.).

62.   Wombwell; Turner. 1892–? (Tr.Dir.).

63.   Worsbrough; Wood Brothers. (SE/357036). 1830–1871. Site abandoned and works transferred to Barnsley, Hoyle Mill, (SE/359063) from 1872–1982. Flint glassworks. From 1834 operated by Wood family. Specialised in lead glass household items with heavy cut decoration in addition to engraved and coloured glass. Later produced light bulbs and chemical glassware. Hoyle Mill works demolished 1982 and site now redeveloped.

SECTION B

The following are occasionally listed in Trade Directories as "Manufacturers" but were cutters and grinders of products obtained from flint glassworks.

1.   Blunn, James, 42 Pond Street, Sheffield
2.   Blunn, Thomas, Harvest Lane, Sheffield
3.   Brown, H., 51 Bridge Street, Sheffield
4.   Chadburn, Rivelin Bridge Wheel, Sheffield (Lens grinder).
5.   Hazlewood, John, Nether Hallam, Sheffield
6.   Jackson, Thomas, 49 Furnace Hill, Sheffield
7.   Jackson, Thomas, Workhouse Croft, Sheffield
8.   Jeffrey, T., Havelock Works, Walker Street, Sheffield
9.   Langwell & Co., Nursery Steam Grinding Wheel, Stanley Street, Sheffield
10.   Lenthall, T., Radcliffe Wheel, Love Lane, Sheffield
11.   Melling Carr, Attercliffe Bridge, Sheffield
12.   Nicholls, George, 10 Norfolk Street, Sheffield

SECTION C

The following are listed in Trade Directories as 'Manufacturers' but the address given refers to administrative offices or warehouses, not production sites.

1.   Birmingham Plate Glass, 27 Church Street, Sheffield
2.   Blunn, James, Pond Street, Sheffield
3.   Branwell, James, 48 Hoyle Street, Sheffield
4.   Butler, Francis, 35 Sheffield Road, Barnsley
5.   Castree & Gee, 77 Arundel Street, Sheffield (Stourbridge glassworks).
6.   Collins, John, 46 Schools Croft, Sheffield
7.   Dixon, Joseph R., 58 Hoyle Street & 26 Matthew Street, Sheffield
8.   Langwell, G., 46 Wentworth Street, Sheffield
9.   Lowe, John, Church Street, Mexborough
10. Mycock, Thomas, 108 Barkers Pool, Sheffield
11. Oxberry, James, 87 Sussex Street, Sheffield
12. Pilkington Bros., 29–31 Union Street, Sheffield. (St. Helens glassworks).
13. Wood Bros., Prideaux Chambers, Change Alley, Sheffield

APPENDIX A

John Houghton – Letters for the Improvement of Trade and Industry
List of Glasshouses in England and Wales – 1696

Account of all the Glass Houses in England & Wales	Several Counties they are in	Number of Houses	Sorts of Glass each House makes
In and about London and Southwark		9	For bottles
		2	Looking glass plates
		4	Crown glass & plates
		9	Flint glass & ordinary
Woolwich	Kent	1	Crown glass & plates
		1	Flint glass & ordinary
Isle of Wight	Hampshire	1	Flint glass & ordinary
Topsham (nr Exon)	Devonshire	1	Bottles
Odd Down nr Bath	Somersetshire	1	Bottles
Chellwood		1	Window glass
In and about Bristol		5	Bottles
		1	Bottles & window glass
		3	Flint glass & ordinary
Gloucester	Gloucestershire	3	Bottles
Newnham		2	Bottles Houses
Swansea in Wales	Glamorgan	1	Bottles
Oaken Gate	Shropshire	1	Bottles & window glass
Worcester	Worcestershire	1	Flint, green & ordinary
Coventry	Warwickshire	1	Flint, green & ordinary
Stourbridge	Worcestershire	7	Window glass
		5	Bottles
		5	Flint, green & ordinary
Near Liverpool	Lancashire	1	Flint, green & ordinary
Warrington		1	Window glass
Nottingham		1	Bottles
Awsworth	Nottingham	1	Flint, green & ordinary
Custom More		1	Bottles
Nr Awsworth		1	Flint, green & ordinary
Nr Silkstone	Yorkshire	1	Bottles
Nr Ferrybridge		1	Bottles
		1	Flint, green & ordinary
King's Lynn		1	Bottles
Yarmouth		1	Flint, green & ordinary
		1	Bottles
Newcastle-upon-Tyne		6	Window glass
		4	Bottles
		1	Flint, green & ordinary
Total		88	

The list is valuable in being the only available summary of the range of the glass industry in the seventeenth century but must be viewed with caution. It is known he missed a glassworks operating in Derbyshire at the time and at least one, perhaps two, in South Yorkshire. In addition, documentary and archaeological evidence shows that, for example, Silkstone produced both flint and window glass which are not recorded in his comments. Other comments may be equally suspect but it is not known on what basis he judged the range of products of the works he listed.

APPENDIX B

SOUTH YORKSHIRE GLASS

SAMPLES OF GLASS ANALYSIS

	SiO_2	Na_2O	K_2O	CaO	MgO	Al_2O_3	Fe_2O_3	PbO	CoO
Silkstone (window)	67.0	9.0	0.5	13.9	6.5	1.4	0.3	–	–
Wentworth (window)	37.7	0.3	2.2	28.5	11.6	16.0	0.08	–	–
Gawber (window)	65.8	7.5	3.5	12.3	5.7	3.9	0.46	–	–
Gawber (brown bottle)	52.9	1.0	2.4	27.2	4.2	7.9	2.4	–	–
Gawber (clear phial)	65.4	4.8	3.9	17.5	4.6	1.7	1.1	0.5	–
Bolsterstone (clear phial)	64.4	6.0	3.7	14.0	4.8	3.1	1.0	–	–
Bolsterstone (brown bottle)	62.2	6.3	4.6	15.5	4.7	2.8	–	–	–
Bolsterstone (green bottle)	62.4	8.2	4.5	13.1	5.8	4.2	0.77	0.4	–
Bolsterstone (amber)	64.5	5.8	5.2	9.2	5.1	1.9	1.2	2.9	–
Bolsterstone (blue)	76.9	15.5	0.6	6.6	–	0.2	0.25	–	0.17
Bolsterstone (Nailsea black)	63.4	6.6	5.4	9.5	4.7	2.7	1.3	1.4	–
Bolsterstone (clear)	65.4	11.4	3.6	1.9	0.2	0.15	0.08	17.7	–
Bolsterstone (clear)	51.0	0.3	6.7	0.2	0.1	0.9	0.22	39.6	–
Bolsterstone (white enamel)	40.7	–	6.8	–	–	0.6	0.3	52.8	–

SiO_2 = silica Na_2O = soda K_2O = potash
CaO = lime   MgO = magnesium oxide Al_2O_3 = aluminium oxide
Fe_2O_3 = iron oxide   PbO = lead oxide   CoO = cobalt oxide

Percentage compositions determined by micro-probe analysis at the Department of Glass Technology, University of Sheffield.

A typical modern composition range for clear glass bottles would contain:
SiO_2 = 69–75% Na_2O = 13–17%   CaO = 9–13% Al_2O_3 = 0.5–2.5%

The Gawber and Silkstone window glass compositions are not significantly dissimilar but the Wentworth imbalance of Magnesium and Aluminium oxides suggests lack of control of the process leading to instability. Colour variations from green to brown to almost black (eg. Nailsea) bottle glass were generated partly by the initial mixture but largely through control of furnace conditions ie. temperature and whether oxidising or reducing conditions in the furnace were dominant. Two types of lead crystal glass were produced at the Bolsterstone works, one having twice the lead content of the other, but both were stable and used for wine glasses, decanters etc. Of particular note amongst the Bolsterstone products was the white enamel glass consisting of 52.8% lead oxide and shows the skiil of the glassmaker in controlling such an unusual mix. This glass was created to melt at a lower temperature than the Nailsea black so that threads could be wound on or worked into the black to create the distinctive Nailsea style.

NOTES

Introduction

1. John Houghton, Letters for the Improvement of Trade and Industry, (Letter 198), Journals of the House of Commons, 11,614; 5 Dec. 1696.

Chapter 1

1. Acts of Privy Council of England, 38,423
2. Patent Rolls, II, Jac I, pt 16, No.4.

Chapter 3

1. BM Straff. MS. 21/69.
2. BM Straff. MS. 20/30.
3. Newent Parish Register.
4. Eccleshall (Shropshire) Parish Register.
5. Ashton under Lyne Parish Register.
6. Ibid
7. Borthwick Institute of Historical Research – Probate records.
8. British Library Landsdowne 913.
9. Borthwick Institute of Historical Research – Probate records.
10. Borthwick Institute of Historical Research – Probate records.
11. Borthwick Institute of Historical Research – Probate records.
12. Sheffield Archives – Sp.St. 64714/3
13. Sheffield Archives – Sp.St. 64714/6,7
14. Sheffield Archives – TC573
15. Sheffield Archives – TC574(a)
16. Sheffield Archives – TC574(b)
17. British Library ADD.MSS.22239.fd.35
18. British Museum Sloane MSS.1351.58

Chapter 4

1. John Goodchild Collection
2. Sheffield Archives – FB153,76/77 and MB 436
3. Thirteenth Report of the Commissioners of Excise: Inquiry into the Excise Establishment and into the Management and Collection of the Excise Revenue throughout the United Kingdom – Glass. (1835)
4. Sheffield Archives – Sp.St. 60651/1

Chapter 5

1. British Parliamentary Commission, 4th Report. (1865). Children's Employment; Glass Manufacture, 20, 332
2. British Parliamentary Commission Report. (1886). Depression in Trade and Industry, 21, Appendix A,74

Chapter 7

1. Extracts quoted from evidence given by witnesses in British Parliamentary Papers
   (1843) Second Report of the Commissioners on the Employment of Children
   (1843) Second Report of the Commissioners on Trade and Manufactures
   (1865) Industrial Revolution – Fourth Report – Children's Employment, Report on Glass Manufacture
2. Wood Brothers papers; Sheffield Archives – anonymous MS
3. Wood Brothers; Sheffield Archives – 358/B5/1
4. *Journal of Glass Technology*: (1931) Vol.15, 233
5. Wood Brothers Day Book; Sheffield Archives – 358/B2/1

BIBLIOGRAPHY

Andrews, C.R. 1950 *The Story of Wortley Ironworks*, South Yorkshire Times.

Ashurst, D. 1970 'Excavations at Gawber Glasshouse', *Post Medieval Archaeology*, 4, 92–140.

Ashurst, D. 1986 'Post Medieval Britain', *Post Medieval Archaeology*, 20, 354.

Ashurst, D. 1987 'Excavations at Bolsterstone Glasshouse', *Post Medieval Archaeology*, 21, 147–216.

Ashurst, D. 1992 'The Silkstone Glasshouses', Old West Riding forthcoming.

Barker, W.R. 1925 'Notes on Some Old Yorkshire Glasshouses', *Journal of Glass Technology*, 9, 322–333.

Brundage, D. 1976 The Glass Bottle Makers of Yorkshire and the Lock-out of 1893, Warwick: MA dissertation unpublished.

Buckley, F. 1924 'Glasshouses of the Leeds District', *Journal of Glass Technology*, 8, 268–274.

Buckley, F. 1925 'The Early Glasshouses of Bristol', *Journal of Glass Technology*, 9, 36–61.

Buckley, F. 1927 'Notes on the Glasshouses of Stourbridge', *Journal of Glass Technology*, 11, 106–123.

Charleston, R.J. 1978 'Glass Furnaces Through the Ages', *Journal of Glass Studies*, 20, 9–33, Corning Museum.

Charleston, R.J. 1984 *English Glass*, Allen & Unwin.

Clark, A.W. 1980 *Through a Glass Clearly*, Golden Eagle.

Clayton, A.K. 1966 'Coal Mining at Hoyland', *Transactions of the Hunter Archaeological Society*, 9, Part 2, 75–96.

Cleere, H. and Crossley, D. 1985 *The Iron Industry of the Weald*, Leicester University Press

Crossley, D.W. 1967 'Glassmaking in Bagot's Park', *Post Medieval Archaeology*, 1, 44–83.

Crossley, D.W. 1987 'Sir William Clavell's Glasshouse at Kimmeridge, Dorset', *Archaeological Journal*, 144, 340–382.

Crossley, D.W. 1989 ed *Water Power on the Sheffield Rivers*, Sheffield University.

Crossley, D.W. and Ashurst, D. 1968 'Excavations at Rockley Smithies', *Post Medieval Archaeology*, 2, 10–54.

Davies,J. 1989 *The Victorian Kitchen*, Guild Publishing.

Deane, P. 1979 *The First Industrial Revolution*, Cambridge University Press

Diderot, M. 1765 'Verrerie', *Encyclopeie au Dictionaire Raisonne des Sciences des Arts et Des Metiers*, 17

Elliott, B. 1988 *The Making of Barnsley*, Barnsley Chronicle.

Giles, C. 1986 *Rural Houses of West Yorkshire*, H.M.S.O.

Godfrey, E.S. 1975 *The Development of English Glassmaking 1560–1640*, Clarendon Press.

Goodchild, J. 1970 *South Yorkshire Journal No.1*, Author.

Gunther, R. 1958 *Glass Melting Tank Furnaces*, Sheffield

Hartshorne, A. 1887 *Old English Glasses*, Arnold.

Haslam, J. 1984 'Excavations at St. Ebbes', *Oxoniensia*, 49, 232–249.

Hey, D. 1979 *The Making of South Yorkshire*, Moorland Publishing.

Hey, D. 1980 *Packmen, Carriers and Packhorse Roads*, Leicester University Press

Hey, D. 1986 *Yorkshire from A.D. 1000*, Longman.

Hill, S. 1982 *Wood Bros. Glass Co.*, MSS, Barnsley Local History Archives

Hodkin, F.W. 1953 'The Contribution of Yorkshire to Glass', *Journal of Glass Technology*, 37, 21–36

Houghton, J. 1696 'Letters for the Improvement of Trade and Industry', *Journal of the House of Commons*.

Hunter, J. 1831 *South Yorkshire*, London.

Hurst-Vose, R. 1980 *Glass*, Collins.

Joy, D. 1975 *Regional History of Railways of Great Britain*, 8, David & Charles.

Kenworthy, J. 1918 'Glassmaking at Bolsterstone', *Journal of Glass Technology* 2, 5–12.

Leader, R. 1905 *History of the Company of Cutlers*, Part 2. Pawson & Brailsford.

Matsumura, T. 1983 *The Labour Aristocracy Revisited*, Manchester University Press

May, T. 1922 *The Roman Fort at Templeborough*, H.M.S.O.

McNair, D. 1982 *Suggested Reasons for the Glass Industry Coming and Becoming in South Yorkshire*, MS, Barnsley Local History Archives

Mitchell, G.H. ed 1947 *Geology of the Country around Barnsley*, H.M.S.O.

Morris, C. ed 1947 *Journeys of Celia Fiennes*, Cresset, London

Newton, R. and Davison, S. 1989 *Conservation of Glass*, Butterworth Scientific Ltd.

Noel-Hume, I. 1961 'The Glass Bottle in Colonial Virginia', *Journal of Glass Studies*, 3, 91–117.

Pape, T. 1933 'Medieval Glassworkers in North Staffordshire', *Transactions of North Staffs Field Club*, 68, 72–121.

Peligot, E. 1877 *Le Verre son Histoire, Sa Fabrication*, Paris.

Raistrick, A. 1938 'The South Yorkshire Iron Industry', *Newcomen Society Transactions*, 19, 51–86.

Ruggles-Brise, S. 1949 *Sealed Bottles*, Country Life.

Singer, C. ed 1958 *A History of Technology*, 5, Oxford University Press

Talbot, O. 1974 'The Evolution of Glass Bottles for Carbonated Drinks', *Post Medieval Archaeology*, 8, 29–62.

Taylor, C. 1983 *Village and Farmstead*, George Philip.

Thirsk, J. 1978 *Economic Policy & Projects*, Clarendon Press.

Thorpe, W.A. 1935 *English Glass*, A & C Black.

Turner, W.E.S. 1938 'The Early Development of Bottle-making Machines', *Journal of Glass Technology*, 22, 252–258.

Webb, S. & Webb,B. 1920 *The History of Trade Unionism*, Authors, London.

Wilkinson, J. 1870 *Worthies of Barnsley*, Bemrose & Sons.

Wilkinson, J. 1872 *History of Worsbrough*, Barnsley Chronicle.

INDEX